100 EXPERIENCES OF MODERN KAZAKHSTAN

HERTFORDSHIRE PRESS

HERTFORDSHIRE PRESS LTD © 2016
9 Cherry bank,
Chapel Street,
Hemel Hempstead, Herts
HP2 5DE
www.hertfordshirepress.com

100 EXPERIENCES
OF MODERN KAZAKHSTAN

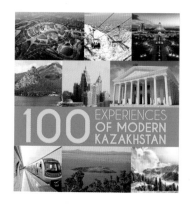

Contributors: Vitaly Shuptar, Nick Rowan, Dr. Kairat Zakiryanov, Rodger Chao, Dagmar Schreiber, Ph.D. Lyuterovich Oleg, Associate Professor Tatyana Imangulova, Senior lecturer Khudaybergenova Nurbibi Musicologist. Honored RK - Aravin Y. P. Kazakh Academy of Sport and Tourism. "Avalon" Historico-geographical Society.

Voronova, Dagmar Schreiber, Natalya Frankovskaya, Michael Kamper, Yelena Kim, Botagoz Krambayeva, Zh. Kairakhanov, Andrey Yurchenkov, Victor Zaibert, Saltore Saparbaev, Alexander Ivasenko, Xander Casey.

Editor: Nick Rowan

Published in partnership with the:
Embassy of the Republic of Kazakhstan
in to United Kingdom.

We express our sincere gratitude to the photographers who contributed their photographs for use in this project:
Vitaly Shuptar, Alexandr Yermolyonok, Mary O'Connor, Aleksandr Petrov, Vera

ISBN 978-1-910886-17-5

9 781910 886175 >

KAZAKHSTAN

Area:	2,724,900 km2 (9th largest country)
Population:	17,736,896 (July 2013)
Capital:	Astana, (Almaty largest city)
Ethnic groups:	63.1% Kazakh, 23.6% Russian, 2.8% Uzbek, 2.9% Ukrainian, 1.5% German 1.4% Uyghur, 1.3% Tatar, 4.3% others
Languages:	Kazakh (national), Russian
Climate:	The Climate in Kazakhstan is continental. In summer the temperatures average more than 30 °C (86 °F) and in winter average –20 °C (–4.0 °F).
Currency:	Tenge (KZT)

Nick Rowan
Editor, 100 Experiences of Kazakhstan
Editor-in-Chief, Open Central Asia Magazine

Foreword

Western businessmen had quietly been building links and investing in Kazakhstan, mainly seeking to grab a share of its nascent but high resource potential oil and gas industry. However, to the ordinary person on the streets of London, Paris, Rome or Washington Kazakhstan remained one of those "Stans," whose name was as difficult to pronounce as its location was to find on the map. By 2006, the country gained unwelcome notoriety with Sasha Baron Cohen's mockumenatry, "Borat", portraying a fictitious Kazakh journalist travelling through the United States and recording real-life and unscripted interactions with ignorant Americans, who were more the focus of mockery than Kazakhstan's portrayal. Despite the initial, and understandable, outrage in Kazakhstan itself, US Kazakh Ambassador, Erlan Idrissov, came out saying that he had found parts of the film funny and wrote that

Twenty years ago, few people in Europe would have been able to name the newly independent Central Asian states, let alone place them on a map. For Kazakhstan, one such state to have gained independence from the USSR on 16th December 1991, the outside world only gave it the faintest of recognition until, in the aftermath of the September 11th 2001 terrorist attacks on the US, western politicians suddenly declared the strategic importance of Central Asia in their war on terror in Afghanistan.

the film had "placed Kazakhstan on the map." By 2012 tourist visas were up tenfold, with the film being credited for helping attract curious travellers to the country.

Today's Kazakhstan can arguably boast a leading position amongst Central Asian nations in the resurgence of importance of former Soviet Republic states. As the world's ninth largest country it is fast shedding its reputation as one of the great travel unknowns as more people explore the great variety of this vast country's attractions. The exotic wilds of the country quickly eradicate the Borat association as visitors find cosmopolitan cities such as Almaty and Astana situated next to the dramatic mountain slopes of the Tien Shan and historical sites of Shymkent and Otrar. The country is fast reinventing itself as a modern nation at the heart of Eurasia with quality hotels, boutique restaurants and a centre of commerce that represents a unique mix of Islamic and futuristic architecture to marvel at.

Geography

Kazakhstan is a landlocked, transcontinental country whose territory covers an area equivalent to the whole of Western Europe. The landscape stretches from the mountainous, populated south eastern regions to the energy-rich lowlands of the west and includes the industrialised north, with its Siberian climate and terrain, through the arid steppes of the centre. It is bordered by China, Kyrgyzstan, Russia, Turkmenistan, and Uzbekistan and occupies a similar strategic position in the history of the Silk Road—as a distant frontier where east met west. For eastbound Silk Road travellers on the direct central route and the longer but easier northern route, this region was the gateway to China.

Kazakhstan is by far the largest of the Central Asian republics, more than twice as big as the other four combined. From its mountainous south-eastern border with Kyrgyzstan and China the terrain transitions to deserts in the central and south-western part of the country and then to the world's largest dry steppe in the north—stretching from the Caspian Sea on the west to the Altai mountains in the east.

History of Kazakhstan

Ethnogenesis, history, culture and spirituality of all the Turkic peoples, including Kazakhs are depicted in Old Turkic Orkhon monuments. These written records fully reflect the spiritual representation of Turks, their understanding of time, environment, quantity, and more important for the analyst, show a network of social relations - the problem of power and control in Turkic Khanate, the restorate of the heroic figures of the Turkic world, reveals the issues of peace and war relationships with sister tribes and enemies.

The latest historical and Turkological literature proves that the ancient Turks had indeed a powerful state, (the eternal el), which was able to resist the Chinese empire, which was reckoned with many medieval states such as the Byzantine, Arab Caliphate, Sogdian state.

In the 8th and 9th centuries, parts of southern Kazakhstan were conquered by Arabs, who introduced Islam. The Oghuz Turks controlled western Kazakhstan from the 9th through the 11th centuries; the Kimak and Kipchak peoples, also of Turkic origin, controlled the east at roughly the same time. In turn, the Cumans controlled western Kazakhstan roughly from the 12th century until the 1220s. The large central desert of Kazakhstan is still called Dashti-Kipchak, or the Kipchak Steppe. The capital was home of a lot of Huns and Saka.

In the 9th century, the Qarluq confederation formed the Qarakhanid state, which then conquered Transoxiana, the area north and east of the Oxus River (the present-day Amu Darya). Beginning in the early 11th century, the Qarakhanids fought constantly among themselves and with the Seljuk Turks to the south. The Qarakhanids, who had converted to Islam, were conquered in the 1130s by the Kara-Khitan, a Mongolic people who moved west from Northern China. In the mid-12th century, an independent state of Khorazm along the Oxus River broke away from the weakening Karakitai, but the bulk of the Kara-Khitan lasted until the Mongol invasion of Genghis Khan in 1219–1221.

The Kazakh Khanate was founded in 1465 on the banks of Zhetysu (literally means seven rivers) in the south eastern part of present Republic of Kazakhstan by Janybek Khan and Kerey Khan. During the reign of Kasym Khan (1511–1523), the Kazakh Khanate expanded considerably. Kasym Khan instituted the first Kazakh code of laws in 1520, called "Qasym Khannyn Qasqa Zholy" (Bright Road of Kasym Khan).

Other prominent Kazakh khans included Haknazar Khan, Esim Khan, Tauke Khan, and Ablai Khan.

Kazakh Khanate was originally occupied the territory of the West Zhetusy, Chu and Talas valley. It combined both moved from the Central and Southern Kazakhstan Kazakhs and local tribes. In the following decades, Kazakh Khanate economically strengthened and expanded geographically. Its territory included a significant part of the territory of the ethnic Kazakhs.

Joining of the oases near Syr Darya to the Kazakh Khanate was the key to the success in the unification of the country by the Kazakh khans. By the end of the XV century, the original boundaries of the state expanded. It includes in addition to West Zhetysu and the above-mentioned cities in South Kazakhstan region, Karatau with surrounding steppe areas, the lower reaches of the Syr Darya and Northern Aral Sea, a large part of central Kazakhstan.

Starting from the mid-18th century Kazakhstan began the process of joining the Russian Empire.

Kazakhstan during the Soviet period

After the Bolshevik revolution of 1917, Soviet power was gradually established in Kazakhstan. The First World War and the Civil War almost totally destroyed the economy of the area. The economy of Kazakhstan only recovered at the end of the 1920s. In 1920, Kazakhstan became an Autonomous Soviet Republic (ASSR) and in 1936 became a Union Republic of the USSR.

Taking into account the economic background of the region, the government of the Union accelerated plans for the economic development of Kazakhstan. As a result, in 1941, the volume of industrial production increased 8 fold in comparison with 1913. Thus, thanks to the ability of the planned economy to concentrate resources on the fulfillment of large-scale economic objectives, Kazakhstan had been completely transformed by the 1930s from a wide nomadic area to a region with a large-scale and manifold industrial complex, a developed agriculture, as well as a high level of culture.

Thousands of large industrial plants, along with tens of thousands of kilometers of railways and roads were built on the territory of Kazakhstan. Kazakhstan became a large producer of non-ferrous and ferrous metals, coal, oil, grain and livestock-derived products. By 1991 Kazakhstan was producing 70% of the USSR production of lead, zinc, titanium, magnesium tin, 90% of its phosphorus and chrome and more than 60% of its silver and molybdenum. Kazakhstan had also become a major producer of grain-crops.

In the late 1970s and early 1980s, the USSR's general economic, social and political crisis also affected Kazakhstan. The rigid system of planned economics was inhibiting Kazakhstan's economic growth and social development. Thus, the USSR's reformist policy, 'Perestroika', was generally supported by the people of Kazakhstan.

Kazakhstan today

During the 24 years of independence, Kazakhstan has taken a worthy site in the world political and economic system, strengthening state sovereignty and territorial integrity. Today, Kazakhstan symbolises stability and tolerance, it has become a reliable partner of the international community and our economy demonstrates high growth rates. The country set an ambitious strategic goal to enter the club of the 30 most developed countries in the world.

Under the leadership of President Nursultan Nazarbayev, over the last twenty years, Kazakhstan has become a centre of regional trade and investment, and became the originator of many international initiatives that provide global peace and stability. Among these initiatives are the Astana Economic Forum, the Congress of Leaders of World and Traditional Religions and International Specialised Exhibition 'Astana EXPO-2017', the theme of which is 'The Future Energy', which is indeed an excellent opportunity for Kazakhstan to showcase not only its unique history and culture but also to demonstrate its achievements, its own innovative strength.

Starting from the early days of independence, Kazakhstan has been an active proponent of disarmament of weapons of mass destruction. The withdrawal of nuclear weapons from its territory, and creation of the ATOM project and nuclear-weapons free zone in Central Asia became Kazakhstan's great contribution to nuclear non-proliferation and strengthening the global nuclear safety.

Kazakhstan is among top ten fastest growing economies in the world. Since independence, GDP per capita has increased fifteen times. With GDP now at thirteen thousand dollars per capita, the World Bank classifies Kazakhstan as an 'upper middle-income' nation. Kazakhstan ranks among the 20 leading countries in attracting FDI. The major part of investments originate from the Netherlands, USA, China, UK, France, Italy, Russia and Canada. These investment statistics demonstrate that Kazakhstan's economy de facto has already become an integral part of the global economy.

How to Use this Book

It is better to see something once, by experiencing, driving and touching it perhaps, than to hear about it a hundred times. However, in the case of Kazakhstan, this famous saying is only half right, because even hearing about Kazakhstan will likely have been a rare experience for many. If you have just bought this book, or are considering its purchase, then try and buy it together with a flight ticket and go to the centre of the Eurasian continent for yourself.

If you are already in Kazakhstan, then begin to read and consider it paragraph-by-paragraph, experience by experience. It goes without saying that it will take quite a lot time to experience everything that Kazakhstan has to offer (one glance at the map is enough to understand why). So, do not be discouraged if after a very intensive month or so in Kazakhstan, you have hardly experienced even a quarter of the feelings, emotions, places or senses described in these paragraphs. Just come back again and keep discovering the country. And even when the time comes that you are able to say that you have visited all 100 experiences of Kazakhstan in this book, you should not think that there is nothing more to experience in this amazing country. Believe us; we are ready to create another book of 100 experiences, because Kazakhstan is so large and diverse that there are at least another hundred experiences that are no less exciting and rich in surprises and your visit to Kazakhstan may just unveil a few more not captured here.

So, go ahead and find out what Kazakhstan is all about!

Country

ASTANA

Astana is possibly one of the fastest-changing cities in the world: if you leave Astana for just a month, on your return you will see changes that would have taken years in other cities. Everything is new: the streets and houses, statues and squares, quays and bridges. The Left Bank, the new administrative and business centre, is where most of the changes are happening and the main attraction point for tourists. Many world-famous architects have contributed: Kisho Kurokawa, Norman Foster and Manfredi Nicoletti are among them. Akorda, Khan-Shatyr, Bayterek, Hazret-Sultan, Pyramide and the House of Ministries are just a few of the sights. Although Astana is mainly a modern city, some traces of it's distant past can be seen there as well. Within the city limits you can the find ruins of Bozok, a medieval settlement. As with any other big and developing city, Astana can be called the city of contrasts, because old, crumbling houses can neighbour modern and luxurious buildings. It is a matter of time, of course, before these disappear.

KHAN SHATYR

Khan Shatyr (in Kazakh - "Khan's Tent") is another dramatic creation of the famous British architect, Norman Foster, that has already become one of the symbols of the Kazakh capital. A huge tent-shaped structure, whose spire rises to 152 meters, it is the largest of its kind across the globe. Khan Shatyr is located at the end of the "Millennium Axis", the central architectural component of the Left Bank of Astana, on the opposite side of which is the presidential residence, Akorda.

Foster, who designed the building, was planning to create an atmosphere of comfort and relaxation from everyday life and the outside world, including extreme weather conditions - very fitting for Astana's unique and, at times, severe climate. Khan Shatyr is the largest shopping and entertainment centre in Kazakhstan. In addition to boutiques, restaurants and movie theatres, there is also something quite unexpected - a beach resort with a truly tropical climate (it is always 35 degrees Celsius). Located here are corresponding tropical plants, sun loungers and parasols, as well as a heated sandy beach from the Maldives and warm water in pools with wave machines.

AKORDA

This building, often carelessly referred to as the "White House of Kazakhstan", is very different in size and proportion to the residence of the U.S. president, but it is the palace and main residence of the First President of Kazakhstan. You will probably not be lucky enough to see inside of this "holy" edifice: Tours of the residence of the Kazakh president for tourists do not happen at all (except for the virtual tour on the official website). So to enjoy the magnificently pompous architecture you must remain on the outside and at a distance. The president has lived here since late 2004, which was when the new Astana residence was officially presented to the public.

Akorda is Kazakh for, "the white headquarter". This was the name of one of the "khanates" formed after the collapse of the famous Golden Horde, which was ruled by the descendants of Juchi, the eldest son of Genghis Khan, the ancestor of the future Kazakh rulers. Akorda is often seen as the core of the modern state of Kazakhstan with the official explanation for the name being that the white colour in the Turkic tradition simply means holiness, goodness, and prosperity.

BAITEREK

Baiterek is one of the original objects symbolising the new capital, and among the most mentioned and replicated on souvenir products. Baiterek Tower has for many years, been the defining symbol of Kazakhstan. Rising to a circular viewing platform from which there is a spectacular view of the new part of Astana, the "Left Bank" it is a must-see part of a visit to Astana. Baiterek has been "implanted" so deeply in the minds of the people, that it in many cities and villages it has been replicated. Do not be surprised, if you see many small and medium "Baitereks" in central areas of villages/towns during your trip to Kazakhstan.

According to popular legend, Baiterek - is the magical "tree of life", found by a hero of a number of Kazakh tales, Yer-Tostik, after a long journey. According to legend, a magic bird, Samruk, every year lays a golden egg in the branches of the tree, and all the dreams and desires of people are hidden in this egg. At 97 metres tall, the tower represents a stylized tree crowned with a huge golden dome representing this egg, which is 22 metres in diameter. One of the favourite pastimes for visitors to Baiterek is placing their hands next to the metallic impression of the palm of the first Kazakh President - Nursultan Nazarbayev, which is located in the panoramic Tower Hall. They also make wishes - and it is said that these wishes will come true...

NORTHERN LIGHTS

The residential complex "Northern Lights" - a bold unique project embodied in the style of Hi-tech, won the International Association of Architects' Union. In this project come together the most advanced achievements in the field of architecture and design, construction and engineering equipment.

Three towers of unusual shape in 33, 37 and 42 floors similar to translating into reality the warm glow of the northern lights, and are one of the most beautiful projects of the capital of Kazakhstan, deservedly attracting the attention of citizens and guests of the main cities of the country.

The project is unique not only unusual shape. The residential complex "Northern Lights" is designed with that in mind that in the Astana harsh winter its residents are warm and comfortable 24 hours a day. To do this, all three buildings united by a large stylobate, which provides a range of infrastructure: convenience stores, boutiques, beauty parlors, coffee shops, banks and more.

EMERALD TOWERS

The complex of three towers of different heights high-rise (37, 40, 53 floors) in Astana. "Emerald quarter" is the tallest building in Kazakhstan.

The concept of a complex designed by architect Roy Varakalli and firm Zeidler Partnership Architects (Canada), in conjunction with the Design Institute "Basis". A feature of the buildings is asymmetric, so starting from the 32nd floor area increases subsequent floors, the last floor is rejected by 15 meters.

The height of the buildings, "Emerald quarter" of 37 and 49 floors. The height of a 49-storey building - 201 meters! Today this building is the tallest building in Kazakhstan. Architecture "Emerald quarter" has many unique features: starting with 32 floors, the area of each successive increases. For example, buildings are asymmetrical with deviating 9 meters top. Massa's tallest building - 186 ths. Tons. At its base are bored piles and foundation slab thickness of about 3 meters.

HAZRET SULTAN MOSQUE

Situated on the Right Bank of Astana, near the US embassy, Kazakh Yel monument and the Pyramid, Astana's main mosque is built of white marble and towers impressively at 77 metres. The name of the mosque, Hazret Sultan, reminds us of the most widespread title of saint sufi Khodja Akhmed Yassavi and, surprisingly, is a part of the Kazakh president's full name. Only since July 2012 has Hazret Sultan taken top spot from Nur-Astana mosque that was previously the main mosque and became the biggest mosque in Central Asia. Up to ten thousand people can pray in its huge territory (of more than 11 hectares) at the same time. From some angles, the Hazret Sultan looks so impressive, that the Pyramid (not a small structure itself) suddenly seems smaller and less stunning. There were even rumors that the National Geographic Channel shot an episode of its Mega Structures documentary about Hazret Sultan, but nobody has seen it yet. Who knows, great structures always attract great rumors.

YESIL RIVER

For its dry and shallow expanses, in the central part of the country, the River Ishim (in Kazakh, Yesil) looks really impressive. In Astana the riverbed has been widened and its banks are encased in granite that gleams in the sun. Ishim's riverside is a popular place among city dwellers and visitors to take a stroll in the evening or go jogging in the morning. One can admire this peaceful scene by sitting in a white fretted arbor on the high bank. You can also use the services of boatmen and discover Astana from aboard. Today, the river is a border between the old and quite simple Right Bank and the new and modern Left Bank, literally between provincial past and new capital gloss. Although, in the area of Akorda and Pyramid, you understand which future is waiting for the whole city very soon: here both the Left Bank and Right Bank are built-up in a modern and original way.

THE LIBRARY OF THE FIRST PRESIDENT

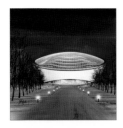

The Library of the First President of the Republic of Kazakhstan – Leader of the Nation was established in March 13, 2014, in order to ensure operation of personal library and personal archive of President, to study history and development of Kazakhstan, as well as promoting the ideas and initiatives of President at home and abroad.

It is the Center of the sitting head of state. In the Library of the First President of Kazakhstan collected more than 20,000 books and 700 exhibits from the personal collection of Nursultan Nazarbayev: gifts of Heads of States, products of art and historical curiosities, acquired at the expense of the President himself.

The Library – is not only a modern electronically archive infrastructure, but also a unique information resource, component of the national cultural and historical heritage. The official website www.presidentlibrary.kz provides access to electronic Leader of the Nation Library. Through an electronic database, visitors are able to get access to the sources of the World Digital Library and the Global Library of electronic journals. Among them, Library of Congress, Library of Oxford and Cambridge Universities, Russian State Library etc.

PALACE OF PEACE AND RECONCILIATION

They also call it the Palace of Peace and Accord. But, to be honest, nobody uses this term. Locals know it simply as Pyramid (because it has the shape of a pyramid). Situated on the Right Bank of Astana, just opposite the presidential residence, Akorda, the 62 metre high Pyramid is one of the most remarkable landmarks of the city. Like a number of other famous structures of Astana, the Pyramid was designed by the famous British architect, Norman Foster. Four sides of the Pyramid are oriented to the face the four sides of the world, this serves as a symbol of friendship, unity, peace and tolerance, which Kazakhstan adheres to. Actually, the Pyramid was built to host regular congresses of leaders of world and traditional religions. But it also has other facilities, including exhibition and conference halls, a huge opera hall, the International Centre of Cultures and Religions and the Academy of the Turkic World. "Besik" Hall, the lightest and the highest part of the Pyramide, is the place, where religious leaders used to meet during the congresses.

11

KAZAKHSTAN CENTRAL CONCERT HALL

The Central Concert Hall is a center for performing arts in Astana, the capital city of Kazakhstan. It was designed by Italian architect Manfredi Nicoletti and was inaugurated by the President of Kazakhstan, Nursultan Nazarbayev on the Nation's Independence Day - the 15th of December - in 2009.

The building's shape evokes the dynmism of a flower's petals as a metaphor for the dynamism of music itself. The building's external structure comprises a series of curved inclined walls made of concrete with a blue back painted glass panels cladding. Those structures protect the building's interior functions from Astana's harsh weather conditions.

The building features a thirty-meter-high foyer which extends over 3.000 square meters, which is intended to create an urban-scale internal public square that could welcome the citizens of Astana throughout the entire year. The building contains three different music halls. It also encloses restaurants, shops, and bars.

EXPO 2017

On November 22nd 2012 Astana was chosen by the International Exhibitions Bureau as the venue to host EXPO-2017, which will focus on the theme of "Future Energy". The theme is aimed at concentrating on both the future of energy and also on innovative, practical energy solutions and their global impact. EXPO-2017 will be the first time that a major international exhibition of this kind is coming to a country from the former Soviet Union. More than 100 countries are expected to participate. Around 2-3 million people are expected to visit the international pavilions from June to September 2017.

Construction on the exhibition grounds will follow the principles of a green economy, using smart-power supply networks and buildings with renewable power sources. This unique and highly advanced building project will spur on the technological development of the country. Not only will the capital get a new district with modern buildings and infrastructure, but also new premises for implementing innovative ideas after the exhibition.

Two bus stations and a railway station are under construction in Astana. Exhibition pavilions and new housing spread out over 173 hectares will be constructed over the next three years, so the face of the city will be completely different by 2017.

ASTANA OPERA HOUSE

The State Opera and Ballet Theatre "Astana Opera" was founded in 2013 on the initiative of President of the Republic of Kazakhstan Nursultan Nazarbayev.

Situated on the left bank of the Ishim River, the Astana Opera House is striking in its splendor. The Astana Opera is on par with the world's leading opera houses, such as La Scala in Milan, Teatro Real in Madrid, the Bolshoi Theatre in Moscow and the Metropolitan Opera in New York among others.

The vestibule, the lobby, auditoriums and the main stage are built in a high-style architectural classicism. The main auditorium seats 1,250 people and the Chamber Hall seats 250.

The orchestra pit is designed for 120 musicians and, if necessary, can be used to expand the stage area.

On 21 June 2013, the opera "Birzhan-Sara" written by the great Kazakh composer Mukan Tolebayev officially opened the first season of the Astana Opera. In the autumn of the same year, the inauguration of the Astana Opera House took place. The theatre was presented to the world community with G. Verdi's "Attila".

14

AIR ASTANA
STOPOVER HOLIDAYS PROGRAM

Air Astana is quietly revolutionizing air travel to and within the vast and mysterious lands that make up Central Asia. From its base in Kazakhstan its modern fleet and award winning service are reviving the best traditions of the old Silk Road. Air Astana now ranks amongst the world's best airlines for passenger service. It became the first carrier from the Russia/CIS/Eastern Europe region to be awarded the prestigious 4-Star rating by Skytrax World Airline Awards and was named The Best Airline in Central Asia and India. Air Astana currently operates one of the youngest fleets on the globe.

To create comfortable conditions for tourists and transit passengers during their stay in Kazakhstan Air Astana has launched Stopover program. Visiting travelers are invited to enjoy the Jewel of the Steppes, Astana and the City of Apples, Almaty. It is a flexible and everyday product – arrive on any Air Astana flight. The program is available on pre-booking at very attractive fare. The Stopover Package provides airport transfer, hotel accommodation, optional sightseeing tour. All details of the program are featured on www.airastana.com/Plan/Stopover Holidays.

Almaty

ALMATY

Population is 1.5 million - Almaty is the former capital of Kazakhstan. It is already more than 15 years since the capital has been moved from mild and soft climate of North Tian-Shan into the cold and windy prairie of Central Kazakhstan. In spite of everything, Almaty is still the biggest city in the country and is the main commercial, financial, scientific and educational centre. Almaty is also the place where the majority of tourists come. The city has always been a good starting point for further journeys and is often included in the itinerary of many expeditions since the 19th century, whether it be Nikolay Przhevalsky and Peter Semenov-Tienshansky, or Ewan MacGregor and Charley Boorman. Explore the historical center with its merchant houses and old churches, visit one of its bazaars, go to Koktobe and Medeo, take a stroll along Almaty Arbat and fling yourself into the local nightlife.

16

ALMATY UNDERGROUND

The first line of the Almaty underground was opened on 1st December 2011. A 2.9-kilometre (1.8 miles), two-station extension of the Metro to Moskva station opened on 18th April 2015. The Almaty underground has a total length of 11.3 kilometres (7.0 miles) and serves nine stations. It owns 28 train cars, which generally operate as seven four-car train sets on the line.

The Almaty underground is the second in Central Asia, after the Tashkent underground in Uzbekistan. It has the beautiful marble floors and various forms of artwork on the walls. With trains arriving every 10-15 minutes, and the temperature below 20 degrees Celsius, this is definitely the way to travel during the summer.

MEDEO

Medeo, located in the Small Almaty Gorge, south-east of the centre of Almaty, became known throughout the world when it was built in 1972 as part of an alpine winter sports complex which sits about 1690 metres above sea level. The ice rink, with an area of 10.5 thousand square meters, is one of best top places to host international competitions in speed skating, hockey, and figure skating. Quite by chance, the strongest skaters of the world have set over 120 world records at Medeo.

Fortunately, the ice rink is open not only for professionals but also for those who want to skate for pleasure, and from November to March this is one of the activities available. The site has a mild climate and good infrastructure for recreation. It has become one of the first places in the outskirts of Almaty to which guests of the city are brought. Another attraction is the Medeo mud dam, which you can climb up by walking up the long "ladder of health," consisting of 837 steps. From the top you can enjoy a stunning view of the beginning the Northern Tien Shan's mountain peaks.

18

SHYMBULAK

The slopes of the ski resort Shymbulak (or Chimbulak) have been famous since the times of the Soviet Union. In 1954, 25 kilometres from Almaty, the resort opened its facilities for skiers. Shymbulak became one of the main training bases for Soviet skiers and its slopes repeatedly held Union and republican championships.

Shymbulak's topography means the ski slopes have a height difference of about 1000 metres. Its highest point, Talgar Pass, is 3,180 metres above sea level, while the base station is located at 2,260 metres. The ski run down from the top of Talgar Pass is 3.5 kilometres, with an average width of 25 metres and a slope of 11° - 29°. These parameters allow athletes to build up quite a speed over the course. The Shymbulak season lasts from mid-November to late March. You can access the base station by using the modern gondola that starts from the Medeo. There are 3 ski lifts from the resort that enable you to get to Talgar Pass. A snowboard park provides snowboarders the chance to show off their tricks. Equipment rental, including skis, snowboards and sleighs, can be found at the 4 star Shymbulak Hotel.

KOKTOBE

Koktobe ("Green Hill"), a small hill bordering the south-eastern side of the Almaty metropolis. It is the most popular viewing area of the city, which is particularly spectacular during sunset and at night. The landscape stretches from Koktobe towards the snow-capped peaks of the Trans-Ili Alatau. Koktobe is also a very popular recreation destination. There are souvenir shops, rides, a petting zoo, restaurants, national cuisine and numerous cafes that allow you to combine culinary pleasures with cultural experiences. And the greatest surprise? A monument to the Beatles!

There is powerful TV tower on the top of Koktobe, some 372 metres tall, which is one of the trademarks of the city (although not a classic view, the panorama with a view of the TV tower is one of the most classic landscapes of Almaty), and another example of seismic resistance. The most interesting way to get to Koktobe is via a cable car that starts near the Palace of the Republic. During the 6 minute journey, you can enjoy the urban landscape with a bird's eye view.

MUSEUM OF FOLK MUSIC INSTRUMENTS

Have you ever heard the names like Konyrau, Sazgen, Zhetigen, Asatayak, no? Then come to the museum and show to your children the folk musical instruments that the museum has to offer. You will be impressed by the new updated and renovated exposition.

For adults and children there is thematic excursion programs, master-classes on playing folk instruments and participation in theatrical performance and concert of the ethno-folk group "Turan".

The museum offers its halls for conducting children's birthday parties. Let your kids not only play with their favorite cartoon heroes, but also commit together with them an entertaining journey into the world of culture and music of their ancestors.

Also the cozy Concert Hall of the museum provides a platform for private concerts, weddings, celebrations and corporate events, national ceremonies, fashion shows, as well as seminars and trainings. There is a lecture hall with subscription programs and special projects for children.

ALMATY ARBAT

Almaty Arbat is a popular destination for rock fans, and in the evenings it is often possible to observe their gatherings for parties. This tree-lined pedestrian street is the first place any aspiring musician comes to busk. It is a favourite place for many groups in Almaty, and other unofficial events such as flash mobs, often utilise this venue. In Arbat, you can buy or just browse the works of local artists and photographers, as well as become a "hero" or a picture of professional photography.

Those who prefer to find art without a tourist bias can find a genuine piece of modern art in the Tengri-Umai gallery, which is located in one of the Soviet towers on the south side of the Arbat. For those who seek a genuine modern Kazakh atmosphere, it is also an ideal place catching up on life's gossip, sitting on a bench and watching the world go by, before having dinner at one of the romantic outdoor cafes, which are also abundant in Arbat.

ZENKOV CATHEDRAL

The Holy Ascension Orthodox Cathedral is, deservedly, considered by many as the most interesting architectural monument of Almaty. The wooden building, rising some 56 meters, was built in the early 20th century, as project of architect S. Tropaevsky by the engineer Andrey Zenkov. The uniqueness of the building was manifested by the fact that it was able to withstand one of the strongest earthquakes experienced by the city at the end of 1910, when almost all of Almaty was destroyed. Remarkably, the only damage suffered by the cathedral was a bent cross on one of its domes. During the Soviet period, the building housed the Central Museum of the Kazakh Soviet Socialist Republic, then it became a concert and exhibition hall, and in 1995, it was returned to believers. After its successful restoration as an elegant cathedral, it now lies at the centre of the 28 Guardsmen Park. This is a very symbolic place, dedicated to the heroes of World War II – the 316 guardsmen of an Infantry Division formed in Almaty, who in the winter of 1941, during the Battle of Moscow, held back the enemy forces but died heroically in battle.

Country

ATYRAU

Located in the west of the country, Atyrau is well-known throughout the world as the energy capital of Kazakhstan. Many major oil and gas companies are concentrated in the city, both domestic companies and famous operators and manufacturers from around the world, including Tengizchevroil, Agip KCO, Chevron Texaco, PFD, Shell, ExxonMobil, WorleyParsons and NCOC.

Atyrau was founded in 1640 and is located in an area of 3500 km², with a population of over 257,000 people. The city is growing and developing day by day: in the past 10 years, the number of residents has increased by 31%, and about 50,000 new jobs have been created.

The Atyrau region possesses a wide range of mineral resources, mainly hydrocarbons produced by oil fields with associated gas. The development and establishment of Atyrau is a key part of the country's oil and gas history. From its roots as a provincial town, Atyrau has become a rapidly growing region, with the production of oil and gas accounting for 40% and 60% respectively of the country's total production.

Atyrau is a modern city with rapidly developing infrastructure and cultural life. It hosts major exhibitions and forums, cultural events, and social activities.

BORDER OF EUROPE AND ASIA

With recent discoveries of Russian geographers, the border of Europe and Asia in Kazakhstan has recently "moved" further to the east from its original location, thus making Kazakhstan a "more European" country than was previously thought.

Many consider these studies rather absurd (and pointless) and not recognised by the international geographical community, so we will continue to stick to the existing definition that has been in place for several centuries. This places the boundary between Europe and Asia in the northern Caspian region that runs along the Ural River. Accordingly, we will assume that being in Atyrau and going from the left bank of the Ural River to the right, or vice versa, will not only move you from one side of town to the other, but also will move you between the two parts of the world - Europe and Asia respectively. To play such a game is quite fun, especially as there are special pavilions on both sides of the bridge with inscriptions for Europe and Asia. Naturally these are popular places to pose for a picture.

25

KASHAGAN OIL FIELD

Kashagan is an offshore oil field in Kazakhstan's zone of the Caspian Sea. The field, discovered in 2000, is located in the northern part of the Caspian Sea close to Atyrau and is considered to be the world's largest discovery in the last 30 years, combined with the Tengiz Field.

It is estimated that the Kashagan Field has recoverable reserves of about 13 billion barrels of crude oil. Harsh conditions, including sea ice during the winter, temperature variation from −35 to +40 °C (−31 to +104 °F), extremely shallow water and high levels of hydrogen sulfide, make it one of the most technically challenging oil megaprojects. Commercial production began in September 2013 and it has been designated as the main source of supply for the Kazakhstan-China oil pipeline. CNN Money estimates that development of the field had cost US$116 billion as of 2012, which made it the most expensive energy project in the world.

SHYMKENT

The third largest city in the country – Shymkent is in the south of Kazakhstan. This is one of the largest industrial and commercial centers of the Republic, located relatively close to the borders with Uzbekistan and Kyrgyzstan, as well as their capitals - Tashkent and Bishkek.

In 2011, Shymkent was voted 'Best City in the CIS', according to the assessment of the International Assembly of Capitals and Cities.

The history of the city totals eight centuries: it is assumed that a settlement on the site of the present city emerged in the 11-12th centuries. The first written mention of the city dates back to the 15th century, when the Persian historian and poet, Sharaf al-Din Yazdi described in his book Zafar Nahme military campaigns of Amir Temur (Tamerlane).

In the 20th century, Shymkent was formed as an industrial center of South Kazakhstan, and in the second half of the century marked a rapid growth. To date, the city has about 70 plants, factories and other industrial enterprises.

Culture of Shymkent grows as well as other areas of life. 19 national cultural centers often organise folk festivals in the parks of the city. There is philharmonic hall, art gallery, museum, library, various theaters, and in 2011 opened a circus.

TALDYKORGAN

Taldykorgan is a modern city in the Almaty region. It is situated in the foothills of Jungar Alatau at a height of 602m above sea level. The Karatal River runs through the city and Taldykorgan is now an important and modern industrial city in the Almaty region. Those interested in the city's history will be interested in visiting the literature museum of Ilyas Jansygurov and the historical and areal museum of M. Tanyshpaev.

Among the places of interest in the city, the Entry Ark and Monument to Kanbabai batyr deserves special mention. Erected on 23rd September 2009 Kanbabai batyr is one of the Kazakh national heroes who lived in the XVIII century. This legendary batyr (strong man) faced off the Jungar invasion of the Kazakh lands. His most outstanding victories were at Lake Alakol in 1725 and Lake Balkhash in 1728.

The Entry Ark in Taldykorgan was built under the project of Architect Temur Suleymanov. It symbolises the main entry to the city, and four supports representing four cardinal points support a shanaryk in the centre – a symbol of solidarity and wellbeing.

URALSK

Uralsk, perhaps, is the city where the history of the foundation of Russian statehood on the Kazakh steppes has been most compactly preserved. In this western city of Kazakhstan, almost everything, including the most interesting buildings in the old part of the city, is connected with the Cossacks and Cossack troops of east Slavic origin.

The Golden Church (Cathedral of Christ the Saviour), has been the unofficial symbol of the city since it was founded with the assistance of the then Crown Prince and later the Russian Emperor, Nicholas-II, in 1891. It was built to celebrate the 300th anniversary of the creation of the Ural Cossack army. The southern edge of Uralsk, which is actually its historic centre, is called the "Kureni"; here almost every house is a monument because much of the area is built in the traditional Cossack wooden log style. Kureni is famous for two things: the Museum of Pugachev and an old church - Michael the Archangel Cathedral. The church was built in 1751 and its walls witnessed and survived the Peasant War led by Pugachev in the early 1770s. The museum of Pugachev is largely a museum of the Cossack way of life during those times.

BOGATYR COAL MINING

The "Bogatir" coal mine, located near the town of Ekibastus, became the largest open-cut mine in the world when it was entered into the Guinness Book of Records in the 1980s having only been opened in 1970. The mine produces 56.8 million tons of coal, despite the fact that the rated capacity of the section was planned only to produce 50 million tons per year. The mine has provided for significant development of the local industry and settlements. In 1987 one of the tallest buildings in the industrial world was built here. The funnel of one of the coal-fired power plants, GRES-2, rising to a height of 420 meters, was also entered in the Guinness Book of Records. Whilst this may not be your usual tourist attraction, it is quite an important part of Kazkahstan's economic development history!

30

ULYTAU

Ulytau (in Kazakh "the great mountain") is one of the great granite masses, which rise suddenly out of the expanses of the flat steppe. In the history of Eurasian nomads, this land has always occupied a special sacred role; some even consider this place "epicentre" of nomadic civilisation. A concentration of mausoleums, petroglyphs, caves, ancient cities and legendary stories create an environment that makes Ulytau the centre of Sary-Arka, and of the whole of Kazakhstan. In recent years, Ulytau was also awarded the complimentary title of "the cradle of the nation". Here Khans have been raised from birth and the headquarters of Kazakh rulers have been located since the earliest of times. The Ulytau mountains are in the geographic centre of Kazakhstan, as if to emphasise their significance. Just south of Ulytau village, the highly visible monument of Kazakhstan People's Unity attests to this importance.

BAYANAUL

Bayanaul is a picturesque corner of nature, at the centre of the Bayanaul region of Pavlodar oblast (province). The village is located near Sabyndykol Lake, at the foothills of Bayanaul Mountains, on the south-eastern part of the Pavlodar oblast. Bayanaul National Park was established in 1985 and the eponymous village is a very beautiful place with a population of just 4,472 people. The area consists of 3 main lakes: Zhasybay, Sabyndykol and Toraigyr. It is set amongst a range of beautiful mountains that attract tourists with their beautiful lakes, beaches, caves and grottos. Every year tourists from all over Kazakhstan come to this place to swim in the lakes and participate in various recreational activities

Nature

BURABAY

Borovoye (in Kazakh - Burabai) is an oasis in the steppes north of the capital, which consists of several large and small lakes (including Lake Burabai), and low, forested mountains. This is a favourite resort of Astana residents who have been building extravagant houses to rest in, away from the hustle and bustle of the city. You can spend days just lying on the beaches and swimming in the lakes. Depending on your interests, you can go for a mountain walk and take in some fresh air or if looking something less strenuous, you can just bicycle on perfectly flat roads. Many enjoy simply doing nothing, enjoying the fresh air of the pine forest. Naturally the area has evolved into providing a mixture of business and leisure activities as well as a medical retreat for recuperation. All of this occurs with the stunning backdrop of the island of Zhumbaktas and the rocky mountain Okzhetpes prevailing over the local terrain.

SNOW LEOPARD

Snow leopard (its local name is "irbis" or "barys") can be fairly called one of the most popular brands of Kazakhstan. Irbis is depicted at the emblem of the main development plan of the country (it is almost used as an official symbol, because Kazakhstan itself is called "the central asian snow leopard"), it is the main part of the emblem of Almaty, it was a talisman of the Asian Olimpic games 2011, there is even a beer made in Almaty and called "Irbis". Look back and you will see, that the hat of the Golden Man of Issyk was decorated with golden images of snow leopards. So, this is the fact, that the Red listed big cat is (and always was) the symbol of high-usage here.

In Kazakhstan you can meet snow leopards in Tien Shan, Jungar Alatau, Saur-Tarbagatai and Altai mountains. The approximate population size of irbis in Kazakhstan is not very big at the moment (about 100-120 units) and poaching still takes place being a serious problem. One of the best places for meeting a snow leopard is Almaty nature reserve, situated south-east of Almaty. Meeting the big cat is definitely hard, as snow leopard is a very cautious animal. So, you should remember, that a good photo always needs a lot of time and a lot of patience.

GREATER FLAMINGOS

Korgalzhyn Reserve, rightly entered in the List of World Heritage Sites by UNESCO, is a unique ecosystem preserved in an almost natural state of the steppes with a variety of large and small saltwater and freshwater lakes. It is also notable that in the largest salt lake, Tengiz, nests a colony of common (or greater) flamingos (Phoenicopterus roseus). The wetlands of the reserve are the northernmost habitats of these species and are the largest in Central Asia. 20,000 pairs these elegant birds nest here. Flamingos can be seen at Lake Tengiz from early May to late September. For the winter, the birds migrate to warmer climes, mostly to the lakes in the Middle East (Southern Turkmenistan, Iran, Iraq, Egypt, Turkey, Afghanistan, and Pakistan).

Flamingo astonish with their simultaneous gracefulness and clumsiness, perched on fragile legs, "stilts". The fact that they live here, in the harsh expanses of the steppes of Kazakhstan, where storms prevail during winter and temperatures can reach as low as minus 40 degrees, should attract even those who are indifferent to seeing animals in their natural habitat.

SAIGA

Sixty years ago thousands of Saiga antelope (Saiga Tatarica) herds migrated to the vast expanses of the Kazakh steppes. These small antelope, that appear more like a sheep on long legs, have distinctive flexible noses that look almost like the head of a vacuum cleaner! Due to their excellent adaptation to the harsh climate of the steppe, these types of animals have lived on Earth since the times of mammoths. However, the barbarous extermination, which began in the late 1890s, has put this species under great threat of extinction (for example, it is estimated that from the original population of half a million animals that once existed in central Kazakhstan, there were only a couple of thousand by 2003). In the end, the species was included in the IUCN Red List and included under protective status by the World Wildlife Fund. In Kazakhstan, the campaign to protect and increase the number of Saiga is making good progress, under the framework of the "Altyn Dala", overseen by the Kazakhstan Association of Biodiversity Conservation (ACBK). Now, the steppes of Kazakhstan are home to the greatest number of individuals - about 80% of the total global population. Three of its major population centres in Kazakhstan are Ural (West Kazakhstan), Ustyurt (Ustyurt) and the previously mentioned Betpak-dala (Central Kazakhstan), which is the largest. According to the latest reports by biologists, there are estimated to be approximately 60,000 Saiga in the steppes of Kazakhstan today.

STEPPE EAGLE

Sitting on the power lines along the roads, on the rocks and mountain peaks soaring above the steppe, Steppe Eagles can be found wherever there is sky and the wind is blowing. Perhaps that is why they bear their name, as they are a symbol of Kazakhstan's steppes. The Steppe Eagle is a rather large bird (with a wingspan of up to 190 centimetres), so it is hard not to notice, even against the background of the boundless steppes.

Often, when filming in Kazakhstan, film directors will start with a shot of this predator hovering over the steppe and seeking food. The image of the Steppe Eagle in Kazakhstan can be found everywhere - from confectionery to beer brands and even on the national flag of Kazakhstan.

BLOSSOMING TULIPS

In the spring and summer, the steppes and foothills of Kazakhstan begin to bloom with all the colours of the rainbow, and the tulips are the reason. Thousands of tourists, eager to capture the tulips' bloom in their memories and photographs, are sent every year around this time into the fields. Tulips can be regarded as one of the main attractions of Kazakhstan. It is in fact the Kazakh wild tulips that have given rise to cultivars, grown for centuries in the Netherlands. Overall, there are 38 species of plants, 18 of which are categorised as endangered. You can arrange to see the different tulip blooms yourself from late April to June in different regions of Kazakhstan. In the Korgalzhyn reserve you can see Schrenk tulips, then to the south of Kazakhstan, in Aksu-Zhabagly and the botanical reserve, Berkara, are Greig tulips, Kaufman tulips and others. The Kolpakovsky Tulip can be found in the Ile-Alatau National Park and the open spaces of the National Park Altyn-Emel, while the virtually extinct Regel tulip, a unique and endemic species, is preserved only in the Chu-Ili Mountains. Beautiful as these flowers are, there is one strict request for the visitor: Please do not pick the flowers as this can harm the bulbs.

APPLES

It is an interesting fact, that Malus Sieversii, a wild apple, native to the mountains of Tien Shan, is considered the ancestor of the overwhelming majority of domesticated apple varieties. The apple is actually one of the main symbols of Almaty and even the name of the city derives from the Kazakh word for "apple" (alma). It's no accident: wild apple forests were abundant in Almaty's surroundings some time ago. The most famous sort of apples in Kazakhstan is Almaty Aport, which appeared in the second half of the 19th century as a result of crossing local Malus Sieversii with imported Aport from the Voronezh region of Russia. Almaty Aport is a very large type (it is not uncommon for them to grow as large as half a kilo in weight). There was a time when the Almaty foothills were rich with apples, but the situation is changing: it is not so easy to buy Aport these days. Apple gardens and forests have become the first victims of thoughtless building in Almaty's foothills and other areas. But far away from the big cities, in other sub-mountain regions, apples are still grown. For some farmers it is their main business. You might ask: why don't they produce cider in Kazakhstan? It's a good question and perhaps they should try!

RELICT TURANGA

Diversifolia Asiatic, also known as heterophyllous poplar (Populus Diversifolia) or Asian Poplar, appeared on earth in the Tertiary period, somewhere between the time when the dinosaurs died out, and the moment when the last ice age began. The characteristic feature of the tree, also known as Turanga, is that the leaves are very different in shape and size, depending on where they grow. They may be tapered, narrow and long, or broad and round. The Asian poplar, thanks to its strong root system submerged in the soil to a depth of 50 metres, is capable of pumping water from the sand and can survive in the harsh desert and semi-desert conditions present in Kazakhstan.

One of the best places to see Turanga is the Altyn-Emel national park, where it forms a large grove of trees. Turanga is also found in Charyn canyon and in northern Balkhash lakeside (lower reaches of the river Tokyrau), as well as a few other places in Kazakhstan, including the Kyzyl Kym, the lower reaches of the rivers Ural and Irgiz.

KATON-KARAGAY NATIONAL PARK

This place is surrounded by legends, it was here a few centuries, people have searched for exorbitant country Shambhala, a paradise on earth, the mysterious land where all the living world is living in perfect harmony with nature.

Katon-Karagay National Park is a treasure of natural and historical sites of the East Kazakhstan district. Its territory is Berel burial ground, waterfall Kokkol, Rakhmanov, and northern branch of the Silk Road. Park is rich in beautiful scenery and unusual natural resources, one of which is the river Belaya Berel, which really like Milk River from a fairy tale, it is white because white clay on the bottom. From left tributary white Berel downstream the Kokkol Falls is formed - the tallest waterfall in Kazakhstan and Altai. The waterfall is 80 meters, width 100 meters. And in Arasan valley, kilometers from Belukha mountains, the waterfall Rakhmanovsky has healing properties.

Katon-Karagay is famous for its abundant wildlife - about seventy species, about three hundred species of birds and dozens of species of fish, some of them - the snow leopard, argaliand others listed in the Red Book of the Republic of Kazakhstan.

BIRD WATCHING

Many tourists come to Kazakhstan, not for its vast steppes or snowy peaks, nor to explore the everyday life of the local population, or for excursions to historic sites, but solely to spend a week or two in its wetlands in order to capture as many birds as possible in their memories and photographs. With 500 species of bird living in (or flying to) the territory of Kazakhstan the country is a haven for all types of birdwatchers who are sure to spot a variety of birds that arrive here for breeding, feeding, resting, or moulting. In places such as the Korgalzhyn reserve or Aksu-Zhabagly reserve, hundreds of bird watchers descend every year, armed with detectors, cameras with long lenses, large telescopes and binoculars, as well as a bit of patience. Although this is a bird's paradise, many often finish the trip also realising that Kazakhstan is an interesting country with a rich history and stunning landscapes.

People

PEOPLE OF KAZAKHSTAN

Without any doubt or exaggeration, the most interesting experience in Kazakhstan is meeting its people! Of course the historical sites and natural resources are important for any traveller, but the people and their attitude always sink into the soul much stronger. Whilst to some, the people of Kazakhstan may seem to be too serious or concerned only about their own affairs, it would be wrong to call them indifferent to the fate of the traveller. Often their concern (some would say - guardianship) may even seem overly excessive, and you may want a little bit more privacy. There is a belief that the hospitality of people is inversely proportional to the density of the population, and it is believed that in the case of Kazakhstan, with its immense and sparsely populated expanses, this is the ultimate truth. The farther away you move from the big cities, the more soulful and touching is local attitude towards the guest. An ordinary tourist becomes a wanderer; a wanderer has always been welcomed and treated properly in the East. At times, the generosity and selflessness of the Kazakh people is truly humbling.

THE ASSEMBLY OF PEOPLE OF KAZAKHSTAN

Kazakhstan is home to over 100 different ethnic groups living together in tolerance and harmony as a result of one of the main tenets of the political system of Kazakhstan. This ensures that the interests of all ethnic groups and the rights and freedoms of the citizens are protected, regardless of their nationality and the Assembly of People of Kazakhstan was established on 1st March 1995 by the initiative of President of Kazakhstan Nursultan Nazarbayev.

The Assembly of People of Kazakhstan is a presidentially appointed advisory body designed to represent the country's ethnic minorities. Its task is to implement the state national policy, ensure socio-political stability in the country and improve the efficiency of co-operation between state institutions and civil society in the sphere of interethnic relations. The APK consists of 384 representatives of all ethnic groups living in Kazakhstan. APK Deputies participate in the legislative process and can propose legislation. APK Deputies elect 9 members to the Majilis (lower chamber of Parliament) of Kazakhstan.

THE BOLASHAK SCHOLARSHIP

Bolashak International Scholarship was established on November 5th 1993 by the Decree of President of the Republic of Kazakhstan, Nursultan Nazarbayev.

At the dawn of independence, the Republic of Kazakhstan needed highly-qualified professionals capable of conducting further reforms and representing the country in the international arena. Talented youth could use the scholarship to study abroad and in the first years of implementation of the program the scholars studied in only four countries — the USA, Great Britain, Germany and France. Today this has been expanded and throughout the whole period of its existence, the Bolashak Scholarship has been granted to 11,126 Kazakhstan citizens for study in 200 of the best universities in 33 countries.

NAURUZ

In Kazakhstan, at the end of March, when the real heat has not yet started and the cold can return at any point, the Nauruz feast of spring and renewal is widely celebrated throughout the country. By experiencing this celebration you will certainly get your own piece of the spring mood, even if at the time of these events there may be unexpected snow.

The name of the holiday comes from the Persian "Nauruz," which means "new day." In Kazakhstan, the festival is celebrated for three consecutive days, from 21st to 23rd March with the main festivities usually falling on the 22nd. On this day, the main streets of big cities are blocked and scenes, yurts, and swings are installed. The presence of the number 7 is obligatory during the celebration of Nauruz in Kazakhstan. Therefore, on this day, according to Kazakh tradition, a special meal, "nauryz-koje", is cooked in every house, prepared from seven components (water, meat, salt, fat, flour, cereals, and milk).

BAIKONUR COSMODROME

In the south of Kazakhstan, between Kyzylorda and the Small Aral Sea is one of the most advanced technical achievements in the world, the Baikonur Cosmodrome. On April 12 1961, the first manned flight into space was launched from this place. The spaceship used was called "Vostok" and was piloted by Soviet cosmonaut Yuri Gagarin. His journey lasted 1 hour 48 minutes and made a complete orbit of the planet.

Although at the time, Baikonur and the nearby city of Leninsk were "closed areas", today access to this place of technological miracles is relatively easy. Despite this, relatively few people come to see the present launches. Since the launch site is shared by both Russia and Kazakhstan, entering its territory requires the permission of both parties, which is not necessarily a quick process. Witnessing this stunning phenomenon – a rocket launch into space – remains a dream for many people. If you cannot obtain access to Baikonur personally, just watch the film by German director, Veit Helmer, titled "Baikonur" in which the inner workings of Baikonur are shown in great detail.

THE KAZAKHSTAN WHEAT

Kazakhstan is a major producer and exporter of high quality wheat, which dominates the output of its large-scale commercial farms. It is also a major processor, with a milling industry that has been the top ranked wheat flour exporter in the world in recent years.

Kazakhstan is among the world's top 10 suppliers of wheat and is a leader in flour exports, exporting some 8.2 million tonnes between 2008 and 2012 and earning an aggregate of $8.8 billion, more than doubling the 2003-2007 revenue. Traditional importers of Kazakh grain are Russia, Azerbaijan, Uzbekistan, Tajikistan, Iran, Kyrgyzstan, Turkey, Georgia, China, Sweden and Afghanistan. They account for more than 98.8 percent of exports, and will provide ample demand growth for the coming years, according to experts at the country's KazAgro Holding, Kazakhstan's grain industry is stable.

KAZAKH LANGUAGE

Salem
(Hello)

Sau-bol
(Goodbye)

Rakhmet
(Thank you)

The Kazakh language belongs to the Kypchak group of Turkic languages. The group includes the Tatar, Bashkir, Karachai-Balkarian, Kumykian, Karaimian, Crimean-Tatar, Karakalpakian and Nogay languages. The ones closest to Kazakh are Karakalpakian and Nogay. Nowadays the Kazakhs use Cyrillic characters from the Russian alphabet with 9 specific letters added. But it wasn't always that way: Arabic characters were in use until 1929 and the Roman alphabet - between 1929 and 1940. The debate about returning to Arabic characters or the Roman alphabet has been raging since Kazakhstan became an independent state. At the moment, taking into account the latest political statements, the Roman alphabet seems the most probable scenario.

Few Russians speak the Kazakh language and even the Kazakh people themselves don't always know it. The authorities try to introduce Kazakh language into public life, but it hasn't taken off yet. Right now you will definitely survive without Kazakh in Almaty or Astana, but visit a small village somewhere in South Kazakhstan and you will realise that just a few words are useful. Try to start with a couple of words and repeat them. "Salem" (hello), "sau-bol" (goodbye) or "rakhmet" (thank you) will open the hearts of local people even more.

Аа	Әә	Бб	(Вв)	Гг	Ғғ	Дд	Ее	(Ёё)	Жж	Зз
а	ә	бе	ве	ге	ға	де	йе	йо	же	зе
a	ä	b	v	g	ḡ	d	e	ë	ž	z
[a]	[æ]	[b]	[v]	[ɢ]	[g]	[d]	[i̯ə]	[jo]	[ʒ]	[z]

Ии	Йй	Кк	Ққ	Лл	Мм	Нн	Ңң	Оо	Өө	Пп
ый/ій	қысқа и	ка	қа	эл	эм	эн	эң	о	ө	пе
i	j	k	ķ/kh	l	m	n	ṇ	o	ö	p
[əj/əj]	[j]	[k]	[q]	[l]	[m]	[n]	[ŋ~ɴ]	[u̯ʊ]	[yʉ]	[p]

Рр	Сс	Тт	Уу	Ұұ	Үү	Фф	Хх	һһ	(Цц)
эр	эс	те	ұу/үу	ұ	ү	эф	ха	һа	це
r	s	t	u	ū	ü	f	x	h	c
[ɾ]	[s]	[t]	[w/ʊw/ʉw/ əw/əw]	[ʊ]	[ʉ]	[ɸ]	[χ;q]	[h]	[ts]

(Чч)	Шш	(Щщ)	(Ъъ)	Ыы	Іі	(Ьь)	(Ээ)	Юю	Яя
че	ша	ща	Ъайыру	ы	і	Ьжіңішкелік	э	йу	йа
č	š	šč	белгі	y	ī	белгі	è	ju	ja
[tɕ]	[ʃ]	[ɕ]	''	[ə]	[ə]	'	[e]	[ju/jy]	[ja]

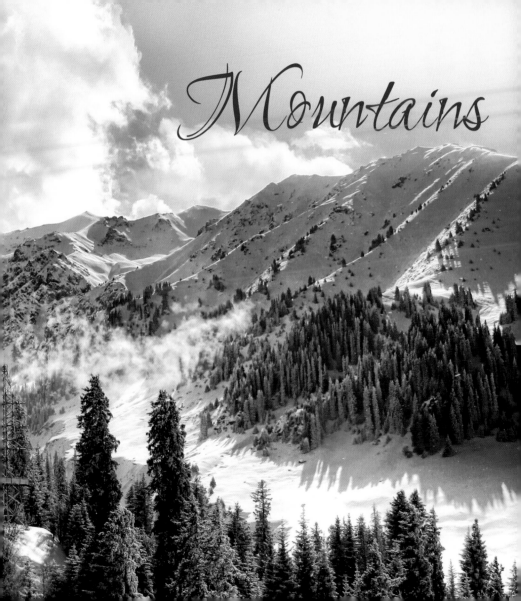

Mountains

KHAN-TENGRI

In the mountains of the Central Tien-Shan, on the border of three countries - Kazakhstan, Kyrgyzstan and China – lies the Tengri-Tag ridge, with its highest point the legendary and sacred mountain of Turks Khan-Tengri (6,995 m). It is the dream of many climbers.

The name is Mongolian and means "Lord of the sky". Kazakhs and Kyrgyz also commonly refer to it to as the "Kan Tau", which literally means "Bloody Mountain" because at sunset the upper part turns almost red. Mixed with the shadows from the clouds, the mountain creates the illusion of streams of scarlet blood flowing down its sides. The perfect pyramid that caps Khan-Tengri makes it look like the highest peak in the Tien Shan and for many years this was believed to be the case. Only in the 1950s was it proved that the height of Khan-Tengri Peak is 400 metres lower than Pik Pobedi (Victory Peak). The first explorers to summit the mountain were Mikhail Pogrebetskiy, Boris Tyurin and Franz Zauberer who ascended Khan-Tengri from the Kyrgyz south side on September 11, 1931.

BELUKHA

The Altai Mountains and its highest point - Mount Belukha - have attracted travellers from all over the world for many years. This eternally snow-capped mountain is a magnet for admirers, known as the gateway to the world of gods, the legendary Shambhala. Located on the border of Russia and Kazakhstan, crowning the Khatun Ridge, the eastern peak of Belukha rises above sea level to a height of 4506 metres. Symbolically, the mountain's two-headed peak resembles a saddle and many attribute this to the reason behind the special veneration of the mountains by ancient people. After all, Altai was the cradle of ancient nomads, who subsequently spread all over the Eurasian continent.

The most famous admirer of Belukha was the philosopher and artist Nicholas Roerich. Enchanted by the Altai mountains, Belukha, its mysteries, caves and meadows, Roerich depicted the surrounding landscape in his paintings, allowing the mountain range to become known across Russia and abroad. Despite this fame, the summit seemed insurmountable until 26th July 1914, when two brothers, Boris and Mikhail Tronovs, became the first to successfully ascend it.

51

SHERKALA MOUNTAIN

Sherkala Mountain, which is located near the Shayir settlement, is regarded as both a natural and historical landmark. It is a 300 metre high remnant of miraculous shapes, resulting from elevation of the land from the ocean depths. People say that the mountain resembles an inverted leech, yurt or sleeping lion in shape.

Sherkala means "tiger-city" in Farsi and there is a belief that the mountain has taken this nickname due to the bravery of its residents who live at the foot of the mountain. During enemy attacks, they went to a stronghold on the hill and defended from here. An ancient well at the top of the mountain has been found, which confirms this theory. There are also caves in the rock where most people are afraid to go because there is a belief that the last defenders of the mountain stronghold hid in these caves while retreating and have stayed there ever since.

Not far from the mountain, there are excavations of the ancient site of Kizil-Kala, which was the largest city and a caravanserai in the littoral lands of Caspian in the Middle Ages. It stood on a branch of the Silk Road that led to Astrakhan on the northern part of the Caspian Sea.

AKTAU MOUNTAINS

The Aktau Mountains ("white mountains" in Kazakh), are located in the eastern part of the Altyn-Emel national park. Contrary to their name, these ancient mountains are not really white. They can be purple, brown, green, blue, or any other colour. Some of them do, however, become a dazzling white but only in the direct rays of the midday sun. In these mountains, there are many manmade architectural relics. Watchtowers, colonnades, and fortress walls of a medieval town can be made out, the once sharp edges of their walls abraded over many centuries. This splendour, which does need a little imagination, is the product of time and the unpredictable outcome of the wind, and rain.

53

BEKTAU-ATA

About 70 kilometres north of the city of Balkhash is one of the most remarkable places in North Balkhash – the mountain oasis Bektau-Ata, whose highest peak is a reference point for an expanse of land that is largely untouched by humans and full of natural diversity. The highest point of the mountains, the Bektau-Ata peak, reaches 1,214 metres above sea level, and its height from the top to bottom is about 600 metres.

Bektau-Ata is an un-erupted volcano, geologically known as a pluton, where sub-volcanic lava has hardened and formed a series of cracked dikes that permeate the mountain Over thousands of years, weathering processes have carved the granite into a series of true works of art – a series of bizarrely shaped rocks that people have given strange names to such as, "mushroom", "chest", "turtle" and "triple-tooth". On one of the slopes of the mountain range is a legendary cave with a spring that people believe has curative water. It is believed that the ancient Turks carried out sacrifices to the goddess of fertility here. To this day the cave is considered viviparous and childless women come here to seek help.

KARAGIYE DEPRESSION

In the western part of the Mangishlak plateau, about 50 kilometres from the city of Aktau, stretching for over 40 kilometres from north-west to south-east is one of the deepest depressions in the world. At its lowest point it is 132 metres below sea level. Karagiye, derived from Turkish, means "black mouth". The formation of the depression is believed to be associated with the leaching of salt from the rock, subsidence and karstic processes that took place on the coast of the Caspian Sea, giving rise to fissures and sinkholes. These processes continue today, as evidenced by the cliffs and escarpments dissected by broad and deeply eroded gorges. A few years ago scientists conducted research in Kazakhstan, discovering that an almost waterless Karagiye was a natural generator of rain clouds. Ascending air in the summer cools and forms many kilometres of rain clouds over the depression. This occurrence is confirmed by satellite images obtained from space. The basin also has the reputation as an abnormal site where it is possible to see unidentified flying objects or encounter other paranormal phenomena.

CHARYN CANYON

It is often said that the Charyn (Sharyn) Canyon of Kazakhstan is a miniature version Colorado's famous Grand Canyon. This national park, located along the river Charyn (Sharyn), which is one of the tributaries of the river Ili, is among the most popular and most visited places in the country. But unlike its bigger brother in the United States, this is not the Wild West, but the Wild East. Its takes some adventure to get as far as the canyon though if coming from Almaty. Charyn Canyon is located on the border with China, some 200 kilometres from Almaty, and is accessible only with your own transport and over very poor roads. However, it is worth the uncomfortable ride to experience Kazakhstan's "Grand Canyon", stretching for 154 kilometres. Visitors are rewarded with exceptionally intricate canyon arches and caves up to 300 metres high, surrounded by steep slopes and jagged columns. These unusual rock formations, created by nature over thousands of years, are all too reminiscent of fairy tales, which is why different parts of the canyon have been assigned poetic names such as the "Valley of Castles" (the most popular area of the canyon) and the "Gorge of Witches."

The rocky cliffs of red sandstone are always beautiful early in the morning, at dusk, and at night under the moonlight. It is particularly beautiful in the spring, when the desert blooms, in the hot summer, under the hum of cicadas, and in the fall when the old trees along the river drop their leaves into the river, turning it a frothy gold. In the winter the white snow creates a graceful contrast with the red rocks.

ASSY PLATEAU

Assy plateau is known for being the place where, in summer, you can be guaranteed to encounter the shepherds with their flocks of sheep and herds of horses, as well as seeing their yurts. These alpine meadows have been used since ancient times as "zhailau", which translates in English to the summer pastures. You can get a sense of what it might be like to live as a Kazakh herder on this mountainous plateau, situated at an altitude of 2800-3200 metres above sea level in the eastern part of the Trans-Ili Alatau. The most common impression visitors have when they look at the local scenery is the scale of its vastness and space. Giant green meadows stretch out ahead, the white yurts are dotted into the scene and animals graze peacefully surrounded by snow-capped peaks, which provide the perfect backdrop for this beauty. Such is the breadth of the scene that it is difficult to capture all the detail in one shot.

In the vicinity are Saki mounds, Turkic stone sculptures and rock paintings from different periods that have provided archaeologists and historians much information on nomadic life and culture. In the south-western part of the plateau is an astrophysical observatory for star-gazing enthusiasts.

BOZJIRA

The most remote area from human civilisation in Kazakhstan is reserved for a part of Ustyurt that contains several hundred kilometres of eroded chalky valleys some 300 meters high that form a plateau. It is the habitat of the Ustyurt mouflon, Turkmen owl, honey badger and other rare desert animals. Reaching Ustyurt is complicated as there are no roads and the lunar landscapes require sturdy off-road vehicles. The special thrill of Ustyurt is Bozjira, two limestone "tusks", that are best observed from a nearby hill. White shades of limestone colour the entire valley with a snow-like effect. The unending maze of towers, canyons and architectural forms make for an easy location to get lost in and show just how strong nature can be in shaping the planet.

58

SPHERICAL CONCRETIONS IN THE "VALLEY OF BALLS"

In the Mangystau region, surrounding the village of Shaiyr, the Sherkala mountain and the Zhingildi tract, there lie an astonishing number of bizarre stone balls scattered across the landscape. These spherical mysteries, which can be up to 3 metres in diameter, look like giant unexploded comets from another world or the cannon balls of giants. They are in fact the Earth's creation, although scientists have never agreed their age or true origin. These so-called concretions, probably 120-180 million years old, may have been derived from underwater deposits in the ancient Tethys Ocean, especially from clays or siliceous flows. In the deep water, a thin surface layer of sediment formed in an area of oxygen-bearing red clays before being compacted by subsequent sediment. In these layers iron and manganese minerals precipitated into the space between the sediment grains forming a cement, or crust. Over a long time these layers grew and gradually became spherical or ovoid in shape, sometimes incorporating the fossils of marine life that provides great paleontological and geological interest.

AKSU RIVER CANYON

Aksu Canyon is one of the most spectacular places of Aksu-Zhabagly, the oldest protected area in Kazakhstan, founded in 1926 in the mountains of Western Tien Shan. Aksu is one of the largest and deepest canyons in Central Asia. Its depth ranges from 300 to 500 metres, while its width spans across 800 metres with a length of more than 30 kilometres. The descent into the canyon is quite complex and steep banks make it impassable in some areas. The sun-warmed rocks and river Aksu provide humidity and create the microclimate of a natural greenhouse in the canyon. The upshot of this is that there are some ancestral plants from bygone eras such as horsetails and ferns. When visiting, take a deep breath and inhale the incomparable flavour of the long-boled junipers. From April to June the gorge is a magnet for botanists from all over the world, because there are many flowering plants typical for Aksu-Zhabagly: Greig and Kaufmann Tulips, *Eremurus lactiflorus*, Karatausky onions, *scilla puschkinoides*, and a variety of wild fruit trees including apples, almonds, pears and cherries.

BURKHAN BULAK

Burkhan Bulak, the highest waterfall in Central Asia, is located in the spurs of Jungar Alatau, in the south-east of Kazakhstan. Situated in a picturesque valley of the river Kora, the waterfall precipitates gallons of icy water from a height of 112 metres. The name of the waterfall suggests that this place has long been sacred for the mountain people because "Burkhan" in Mongolian means "Buddha". That's why many people think that somewhere in the surrounding mountains, not far from the waterfall, there was an image of Buddha. Some people still believe it exists, hidden from sight by the lush vegetation. To experience the true magic of the falling water, you can climb a little higher along the path that clings to the right hand side of the cliff and witness several multi-coloured rainbows shimmering in the mist of the spray.

KIYN-KERISH

Kiyn-Kerish is located 30 kilometres from the shore of Lake Zaisan and is also known as "The City of Ghosts," "The City of the Dead," "Flaming Cliffs," and "Martian Landscape." Many epithets are used to describe this miracle of nature. In fact, Kiyn-Kerish was uncovered by erosion sediments of red, orange, and white tertiary clays, which, being washed by water and blown by the wind for thousands of years, formed this unique and quaint scenery. Trapped within the remaining sediment rocks of Kiyn-Kerish are the remains of ancient vertebrate fauna including rhinos, crocodiles, turtles, salamanders, and other inhabitants of sub-tropical forests, as well as flora such as prints of palm trees, magnolias, araucaria, ginkgo, sycamore, oak, elm and chestnut.

Some see ancient cities and fortresses in the cliffs; in the precipices of the walls and towers, some see ships and yurts. In addition, in the late afternoon, the cliffs of Kiyn-Kerish mostly resemble flames bursting in the wind. It is a surreal feeling to stand there amongst the strong heat that prevails in the tract coupled with virtually a complete absence of water and winds of immense power that dominate the desert plains

62

PLATEAU AKTOLAGAI

This chalky white plateau protrudes from the earth a few hundred kilometres from the border of the Atyrau and Aktobe regions and in the northern extension of Ustyurt, once a seabed. The abundant fossilised remains of shellfish, corals, sea urchins, and other marine life that lived millions of years ago can be clearly seen there. The teeth of ancient sharks, bones of ichthyosaurs (giant marine reptiles) and dinosaurs, petrified trees and plants of unknown species that can be found today attest to an unparalleled diversity. Looking out over the area, it is hard to believe that life once thrived and developed here. Today Aktolagai impresses with its desolate landscape, where the wind whistles ferociously over the desert and saline lands. Amongst the picturesque view of the white rocky outcrop there is only a handful of vegetation that provides precious shade from the glaring sun. Those who visit this solitary place look for silence and space among the untrodden paths of adventure.

KOK-ZHAILAU

The spacious alpine Kok-Zhailau meadows, located neatly between the Big and Small Almaty gorges have traditionally been a favourite year-round vacation destination for those Almaty residents who are not strangers to mountain hikes and picnics in the open air. By happy coincidence, Kok-Zhailau, until recently, was left untouched by construction aimed at "civilising the mountains" and remained virtually the last unspoiled piece of nature close to the city.

149

Lakes

ALAKOL

Alakol, spread out a little east of Lake Balkhash, near the "Jungar Gates" and the border with China, is expected to be the jewel of a future tourist centre. This salt lake in a lunar landscape is located in the cleanest region of Kazakhstan; it is not affected by industrial and other human activities. Despite the fact that in winter the temperature frequently drops to 30 degrees below zero, this vast lake, 54 metres deep, enjoys summer temperatures of over 30 degrees Celsius. The water contains significant amounts of trace elements, which are believed to have healing properties that help bathers to get rid of various ailments. Small stony beaches provide perfect resting places on the banks of Alakol.

Within Alakol's area, in this area 20-30 kilometres from the shore, there are several islands, the largest and most important of which is the island Ulken Araltobe (also known as Stone). On this island the rare Alakol relict gull (Larus relictus) breeds. Access to the island is not open to all, however, as it is part of the territory of the Alakol Reserve.

AK-ZHAIYK RESERVE

This reserve, which is located at the place where the Ural River flows into the Caspian Sea, is one of a handful of global conservation areas providing a wetland habitat for migratory birds. The significance of the Ural River delta is, in particular, the fact that this area is an important area for migratory birds who fly the Siberia to East Africa route. Here, visitors will often see pink flamingos, Dalmatian pelicans, spoonbills, ibis, and other rare and endangered species of avifauna, not to mention the numerous ducks, geese, and swans. However, the Ural River delta is not only valuable for birds, it also hosts a unique and now endangered sturgeon species, the Russian beluga sturgeon, highly sought after in Moscow and the rest of the world for its buttery-flavoured caviar eggs. Finally, the reserve is also home to the Caspian seal, a species who, by its very existence, has shown links that prove the Caspian Sea was once part of the ancient Tethys Ocean that covered the area.

LAKE ZAISAN

Lake Zaisan in East Kazakhstan is widely regarded as a mystical place. This is largely due to an interesting natural phenomenon: with the onset of darkness, melodious sounds over the water surface can be heard, like humming wires. The mysticism and antiquity of Zaisan can clearly be felt in Cape Shekelmes. Looking at its layered colours and surreal landscape, it is easy to imagine how dinosaurs and woolly mammoths roamed the banks of this lake.

It is believed that hundreds of millions of years ago a meteorite fell, turning the solid earth inside out and raising ancient rocks to the surface. The layered mountains, whose multi-coloured layers slant awkwardly, are considered by many to confirm this theory. You can collect your own souvenirs on the coast of Zaisan such as polished stones, whose layered design conveys a miniature characteristic of the local rocks and whose smooth surface is the result of thousands of years of action by the waves of the lake. But please do not take too many of these natural gifts with you; you should also think about those who will be here after you – a couple of photos is probably enough of a souvenir.

KAINDY LAKE

Kaindy Lake is a 400 metre long lake in Kazakhstan's portion of the Tian Shan mountains, located 129 km from the city of Almaty. The lake was created after an earthquake in 1911 that triggered a large landslide blocking the gorge and forming a natural dam. Subsequently, rainwater filled the valley and created the lake.

The lake is famous for its scenic beauty, particularly the submerged forest and the imposing trunks of spruce trees that rises out of the lake water. Above water, the sunken trees appear as large masts from lost ghost ships or perhaps the spears of a mysterious army hiding and waiting for the right time to emerge.

The water is so cold (even in summer the temperature does not exceed 6 degrees) that the great pines still remain on the trees, even 100 years later. Because of the clear mountain water, you can see deep into the depths of the lake. In winter, the surface of the lake freezes over and during this time, Lake Kaindy becomes a great spot for trout fishing and ice diving.

68

KOLSAI LAKES

Kolsai is a system of three lakes located in the mountains of the Northern Tien Shan, 300 kilometres away from Almaty. The lakes are a kind of "cascade", one after the other, in the huge mountain gorge of Kungei Alatau, surrounded by alpine meadows and pine forests. The highest of the lakes is at an altitude of about 2,700 metres above sea level. The usual tourist itinerary includes a visit to all three lakes, with access to the highest of these, which is close to the Sary-Bulak Pass. The Saty village, which is not far from the first Kolsai Lake, is one of the best examples of Kazakhstan's ecotourism development, based on engaging the local communities to open up to foreign visitors and share their unique perspective. The system of guesthouses, which was started about 10 years ago, is open to both foreign and Kazakh tourists improving the well-being of the local community and its individual members. The tour of the lakes and trails usually takes two to three days and it is possible to set up camp by the calming dark blue waters of the lake.

LAKE BALKHASH

To the southeast of Karaganda and north of Almaty, at the junction of the Karaganda and Almaty regions, sits Lake Balkhash, one of the largest lakes in the world (comprising approximately 18,000 square kilometres). The uniqueness of Balkhash is that half of it contains fresh water whilst the other half contains salt water. The eastern end is salty while the western parts are freshwater and the lakes are separated by a narrow strait, Uzin-Aral. The depth of Lake Balkhash does is just under 26 metres and it stretchesfor more than 600 kilometres. Unfortunately, the presence of the Balkhash Mining and Metallurgical Plant in the city means that only an area at considerable distance from the city, on the north shore of the lake, is suitable for visitors to relax. Away from the niose of the city and the roads, a trip to such a remote place will be remembered as a real adventure. One of the nicest places to stay is the secluded peninsula Baigabyl, located 140 km east of the city, in the saline part of the lake. The surrounding scenery is striking due to the purity of its water that glistens back at you with an invitingly pleasant turquoise colour.

SHALKAR LAKE

Shalkar Lake is situated in the Terekty district, 75 km to the southeast of Uralsk. This lake is the deepest and largest reservoir in the West Kazakhstan region and has been attracting people's attention for many years. In ancient times the Oguz, Pecheneg and later Kypchak and Turkic tribes inhabited its shores and tehse tribes were the ancient ancestors of the Kazakhs.

Today the oval Shalkar Lake is some 18 km long and 14 km wide with a depth of 18 metres. The lake's volume is about 1.4 billion cubic meters of water and covers an area of 24,000 hectares. Shalkar Lake's water is very mineral and salty, so hosts a variety of marine life. Fed by tributary rivers to the east, Isen Ankaty (the Big Ankaty) and Sholak Ankaty (The Small Ankaty), and with the Solyanka river flowing out to join the Ural River, the lake's history and tranquility should not be missed.

LAKE INDER

The water in Lake Inder and the nearby caves and hollows in the northern Atyrau region - is brackish (salty) and therefore is believed to have healing properties. The lake is fed by 10 salt springs, from which the most beneficial to health is Aschybulak, located on the northeast coast. You can see numerous "baths" in which people take water and mud treatments. Often there are specimens of ancient fossils - sea urchins, shells and coral – that can be discovered. In addition, a tour to the nearby Inderborsk mine, which is located at a depth of 300 metres, and has a length of 30 kilometres, will take you right under lake Inder into an underworld of salt production and mineral mining. Due to the sterility of air, impregnated with salts, staying in the mine also provides a healthy environment. Added to this, the multi-coloured walls of rock salt provide a quite incredible backdrop to one cave that has been converted into a glistening underground palace.

LAKE SHAITANKOL

The Karkaraly Mountains are regarded as one of the most popular holiday destinations for the past few decades in Central Kazakhstan. In addition, the most amazing and beautiful of these destinations is Lake Shaitankol (or "Devil's Lake" in Kazakh). The lake is too cold to swim in and there is no sandy beach, but amidst its beauty there are also many ancient legends. Usually the legends tell of an unrequited love that ended tragically in or near the lake. Many people comment that you feel a certain mysterious and mystical atmosphere produced by the noise of the pine trees and precipitous cliffs nearby. Animals, in particular, exhibit odd behaviours as a result and can often be heard whining or are seen becoming strangely excited. Tourists rarely stay here for the night, and those who dare often return with stories of unusual things that occurred on the lake during the dark.

SUNSET ON THE CASPIAN SEA

The Caspian Sea is a sea in name only. Although it covers an area of 371,000 square kilometres and is salty, it is actually considered a lake, and the largest in the world at that. The lake inherited the word "sea" in its title from ancient times when it was once called the Southern Sea, then Hirkanian after Khvalynsky or Khazar. Its modern name was given to it by the Caspian tribes who used to live on its coasts as far back as the time of Christ's birth.

Anybody who stumbles across the Caspian Sea should enjoy the surf and sea breeze, with swimming usually possible between May and September without needing a wetsuit. And then after a hard day's activities you can watch the sun setting into its waves in the west with a cold drink from a dozen sites in the city of Aktau.

IMANTAU LAKE

Imantau Recreation Area is a natural oasis, which stretches from north to south for 70 km from east to west 65 km. The basis of it is mountain-forest with ponds and a lake Imantau, which is considered one of the most beautiful lakes in the region. Imantau - natural monument of national importance. An aerial view of the island has the shape of a heart. The island is covered with rare for the area of the Cossack juniper bush, which grows on the coast of the island and gives it a unique look.

The lake water is fresh. The lake with the southern and eastern shores of the river flow and Snake Osipovka. This drain water lakes and Baisary Isbachka. In the midst of a picturesque lake, forested small island in the form of heart. The lake bottom smooth. Beaches on the south and north side of the sand, in the south-west and east - rocky.

Woods in a combination with lakes create a special microclimate. It is home to elk, deer, badgers, foxes, squirrels, grouse, quail and other species of animals and birds.

LAKE MARKAKOL

Markakol has been deemed the blue pearl of the Altai Mountains. Located at an altitude of 1,485 metres and surrounded by Kurchum ridge and Azutau ridge, it is the centre of the Markakol reserve. With an area of 455 square kilometres, its maximum depth reaches 27 metres. Ninety-five watercourses flow into the lake and only one full-flowing river, the Kaldzhir, flows out. The picturesque environment of Markakol, surrounded on all sides by luxuriant mountainous vegetation, is a good backdrop for both a relaxing or active holiday. Many have noted an amazing variety of colours and beauty unique to the lake. It can be blue or azure, grey or almost black, silver or greenish. Nature lovers especially enjoy watching the lake in the late afternoon when it takes on a golden hue as the sun sets over the horizon. Before you go, you need to keep in mind that the Lake Markakol district is the coldest place in Kazakhstan. Summers are warm, but never hot. Snow melts only at the beginning of May. The best time for a trip to Markakol is from the middle of August to the end of September.

BIG ALMATY LAKE

The Eastern branch of the Big Almaty gorge, to the south from Almaty, leads the traveller to the Big Almaty Lake, surrounded by mountains covered with conifer forests. These are the Trans-Ili Alatau Mountains, with at an altitude of about 2500 metres above sea level. The panorama from the shores of the lake is charming with the distinct "Peak of the Soviets", the road to the Ozyorniy pass and the spurs of the Big Almaty Peak all reflecting in harmony with the deep turquoise colour of the lake.

Big Almaty Lake, or BAO, which is what Almaty residents call it, was formed about 10,000 years ago by the collapse of the land associated with tectonic movements. You can still see traces of faults and imagine the scale of the ancient catastrophe. In 1977 a devastating mudflow prompted an increase to the security defences of the city, including increasing the height of a natural dam on the Big Almaty Lake by 10 metres. Nowadays, there is a modest hotel of the Tien Shan Observatory next to the lake (formerly the State Sternberg Astronomical Institute, SAI), where, if you are lucky, can look at the starry sky through a telescope.

ЕТ ТЕАТРЫ

Culture

KAZAKH NATIONAL MUSICAL INSTRUMENTS

The most popular traditional instruments are string instruments. First of them is the dombra, the most popular and the oldest Kazakh music instrument. Some argue that nomads have used similar two-string instruments more than two thousand years ago. The dombra is a long-necked lute with two strings tuned in the interval of a fourth or sometimes a fifth. The strings are plucked or strummed by the right hand without a plectrum.

The other instrument playing an important role is the Qobyz, which is a bowed instrument held between the legs. It is made of carved wood for the body, animal skin for the resonator, and horse hair for the strings, and the bow. The Qobyz is said to have been invented by the legendary shaman Qorqyt, long before the medieval ages. The 'Zhetigen' ('Seven strings') could be seen as a member of the cither family, finding equivalents in China, with the strings being divided each in two parts of different lengths, the bridge being movable and consisting of small bone. There is also a plucked lute called sherter.

DOMBRA

Some might say that the sound of the Kazakh Dombra instrument is too plaintive, and only sad thoughts may come to mind when running your fingers over its two strings. However, these days, the sounds and the tunes (which can be very energetic and even fun) are very strongly associated with the Kazakh culture. The Dombra is a long-necked lute that is most commonly found with two strings, although different regional variations sometimes have three. The Dombra has a flat pear-shaped triangular or quadrangular tapered body and neck with frets to aid the musician. Originally lamb or goat intestines were used as strings, but now it is replaced by more affordable and durable nylon. A special style of Kazakh folk art is connected with the Dombra called, "kuy" which is an improvised genre of music. Competitions reward the most talented is and quick-witted people with the instrument.

79

KAZAKH YURT

You cannot claim to know the real Kazakhstan without having visited a real Kazakh yurt (kiz üy- "felt house"). This ancient nomadic dwelling, which is still used today in the life of Kazakhs, is one of the symbols of the country's heritage. Some cattle breeders move to the "zhailau" (summer pasture) in summer and from June to September live in yurts. You can see them in the mountainous regions usually, but also in the Mangyshlak region just east of the Caspian sea. Yurts are widely used as a mobile home during national holidays, including Nauruz and the national holidays in May. Sitting round a low table, draped in colourful cloth eating a traditional meal before sleeping on "tekemets" (felt carpets) under soft "corpe" (thick quilts) is an unforgettable activity to do in Kazakhstan.

The yurt has a spherical shape, which gives it a maximum heat efficiency. It is warm in winter and cool in summer. The wooden frame of the yurt, after it is installed and fixed, is covered with layers of felt that are attached to wooden poles with long cords. The most important part of the yurt is a round "shanyrak" at the top, which serves as the ventilation of the yurt and the exhaust for smoke from the burning stove located in the middle of the yurt. In addition to its practical purpose, the "shanyrak" plays an important symbolic role. It is inherited each generation; the word itself is used with the dual meaning of "hearth" and "home". It symbolises the unity of man with the cosmos. Lying at night under the open "shanyrak" and looking at the stars from the warmth of the yurt is a favourite pastime of many a visitor.

KAZAKH ETHNIC MUSIC RE-INVENTED

The centuries-old way of nomadic life of the Kazakh people has given them a distinctive musical culture. Singing and playing folk instruments were very much a part of life. The most popular instruments were the dombra (a 2- or 3-stringed instrument plucked by hand), the kobyz (with a deck made of leather and strings of horsehair) and the sybyzgy (a reed flute). Singing was usually monophonic and accompanied by the dombra. Other instruments were simply played on their own. There was a dombra in each yurt and amateur music-making was an integral part of people's livelihood. Those who were especially talented and musically gifted became professional artists - itinerant singers - akyns and instrumentalists - kuishi. Thanks to comprehensive financial support by the people and patrons, they had the opportunity to devote themselves solely to art and reached a high level of professionalism.

In addition to everyday music there was romantic poetry, chanting about the natural beauty of the steppes and mountains, lakes and rivers and the world of animals and hunting scenes. There were also epic storytellers, glorifying the exploits of heroes and warriors. Until the 20th century, the magical art of the shamans had existed.

Since the 1930s, ensembles and orchestras of folk instruments were created on the basis of the Kazakh ethnic music. All the riches of the folk musical heritage of the Kazakh people have formed the basis of modern literary culture of modified European genres and forms.

An example of this is seen in the works of the composer, Sairash. The symphonic trilogy "Kazak Eli", along with the author's subtle musical sensations of ethnic peculiarities of the Kazakh melodies, play the pure sounds of these ancient folk instruments in today's music. This combination has the effect of deepening the historical content and importance of the work.

ҚАЗАҚ ЕЛІ

www.sairash.com

ASTANA FOOTBALL CLUB

Football Club Astana commonly referred to as FC Astana or simply Astana, is a professional football club based in Astana. They play in the Kazakhstan Premier League, the highest level of Kazakh football. The club colours, reflected in their badge and kit, are sky blue and yellow. Founded as Lokomotiv Astana in 2009, the club changed its name to Astana in 2011 and is supported by the Sovereign Wealth Fund, Samruk-Kazyna.

The short history of the club already boasts two league titles, two Kazakhstan Cups and two Kazakhstan Super Cups. In 2015, Astana qualified to the UEFA Champions League group stage, becoming the first Kazakh team to do so. Astana played in group C with Athletico Madrid, Benfica and Galatasaray football clubs.

Astana's stadium is the Astana Arena. The stadium has been Astana's home since 2009, when the club moved from the Kazhymukan Munaitpasov Stadium. The stadium holds 30,000 and has a retractable roof.

BARYS ICE-HOCKEY CLUB

Barys Hockey Club is a professional ice hockey team based in Astana, Kazakhstan. It is one of the founding members of the Kontinental Hockey League (KHL). They play in the league's Chernyshev Division of the Eastern Conference. Their home arena is the Barys Arena. Prior to 2015, the team played its home games at the Kazakhstan Sports Palace for 14 seasons, beginning in 2001. The head coach is Yerlan Sagymbayev and the President is Alexander Koreshkov.

The club was founded in 1999 as a member of the Kazakhstan Hockey Championship. In its 10 seasons of national competition, Barys won its two Championships in 2007-08 and 2008-09. Barys joined the newly formed Kontinental Hockey League in 2008. Including most of the top Kazakh players, the club serves as a base club for the Kazakhstan national ice hockey team.

The most successful season for Barys was the season 2013/2014, when it became leader in goals scored, it had the most effective power play, and it won the first place in the Chernyshev Division and the second place in the Eastern Conference. The biggest achievement of Barys in KHL was qualifying for the semi-final of the play-off games in the Eastern Conference.

ASTANA PRO TEAM

Strong steppe winds across Kazakhstan's spacious countryside together with its mountainous terrain combine to produce Kazakh cyclists with international recognition because they always train in a head wind. So, there is no surprise, that Astana Pro Team, a professional road bicycle racing team, are one of the most positive and widely promoted brands of Kazakhstan. Founded in 2007, with the support of the then Prime-Minister of Kazakhstan Daniyal Akhmetov (who was also the president of the Cycling Federation of Kazakhstan at that time), the team has united the best Kazakh and foreign riders. The names of Alexander Vinokourov (aka Vino), Andrey Kashechkin and Maxim Iglinsky began to be famous both in Kazakhstan and abroad, and cycling as a sport acquired momentum in Kazakhstan. Celebrities such as Alberto Contador, Lance Armstrong, Levi Leipheimer and Vincenzo Nibali were invited to the team to make it even stronger. At the moment Alexander Vinokourov, the former rider of the team, is the general manager of Astana.

84

OLYMPIC ACHIEVEMENTS

National Olympic Committee of the Republic of Kazakhstan sent a total of 115 athletes to the Games, 74 men and 41 women, to compete in 16 sports. The nation's team size was roughly 15 athletes smaller compared to the team sent to Beijing, and had the second largest share of men in its Summer Olympic history. Men's water polo was the only team-based sport in which Kazakhstan was represented in these Olympic games. Among the sports played by the athletes, Kazakhstan marked its official Olympic debut in tennis.

Kazakhstan left London with a total of 13 medals (7 gold, 1 silver, and 5 bronze), finishing twelfth in the overall medal standings. This was the nation's most successful Olympics with the most number of gold medals, surpassing its previous records obtained in Atlanta and in Sydney where the nation had won three golds. Four of these medals were awarded to the athletes in weightlifting, which is Kazakhstan's most powerful Olympic sport along with boxing. Among the nation's medalists were weightlifter Ilya Ilin, who managed to defend his Olympic title from Beijing, and triple jumper Olga Rypakova, who became the second Kazakh track and field athlete to win the gold after 12 years. Professional cyclist Alexander Vinokourov, who competed at his fourth Olympics since 1996, won Kazakhstan's first ever gold medal in the men's road race.

85

BESHBARMAK

Vegetarians can skip this page, because it would not be appealing. What is at issue is the main meal of Kazakh cuisine - Beshbarmak (Kazakhs themselves often just call it "yet"), which is made up primarily of horsemeat or mutton. A celebration party cannot be considered a holiday nor its guests important, if there is no "Beshbarmak".

The meat used in Beshbarmak is usually cooked for a long time on a low heat, making the broth ("sorpa") beautifully rich. Meat removed from the finished broth and cut into small pieces, and this time dough, rolled out into the thinnest flat cakes and cut into small squares, is boiled with onions in a broth. Then boiled dough laid out on a large dish, meat is laid in large quantities on top and broth poured upon with onions. At the last moment, eaters served hot broth.

Beshbarmak is usually served in an important ritual, according to the social role of the eaters – first the oldest or the most honoured guests, and then others. Translated it means "five fingers", because it is traditionally eaten with the hands with special parts reserved for the different guests. The boiled sheep's head is usually placed in front of the most honoured guest, while other parts have significance to other attendees with the children receiving the heart and kidneys, for example, which is believed to help them mature.

BAURSAKS

There is nothing particularly complicated needed to prepare baursaks, at least at first glance. The process of frying them is really quite simple, just drop into the pan for a few minutes before removing. The secret to a delicious baursaks, however, is how the dough is prepared. You'd be foolish to compete with a Kazakh chef whose hands might have made tens of thousands of baursaks, so just leave it to the experts.

What is a baursak? It is a small round or square donut with a hollow interior that is cooked by frying it in a cauldron or deep pan. Baursaks for most Kazakhs replaces bread and are served pretty constantly either as a separate snack with tea, where they can be eaten with salted butter or currant jam, or as a supplement to "sorpa" (soup).

KOUMISS

This fermented frothy milk drink of off-white colour and made from the milk of a mare is a rather peculiar experience to taste in Kazakhstan, Don't be put off by the fact that there are often small pieces of fat that can be seen floating in your cup. The sour-sweet and slightly bitter combination is something you will either love or hate!

Horse breeding nomads first engaged in the manufacture of koumiss from the fifth century B.C. and the drink is first mentioned in Herodotus' stories about the Scythians. Koumiss' alcoholic strength varies remarkably from 0.2% to 40%, but it has always been a drink for all occasions for Kazakhs who usually drink it at about 2.5% strength. Koumiss' value lies in its medicinal properties: it is believed to improve metabolism, treat lung and intestinal diseases and cure illnesses of the nervous system. So important is its medical role that there are special koumiss-cure centres in Borovoye and Petropavlovsk.

BLACK CAVIAR

The "Caviar Capital" of Kazakhstan is Atyrau (which is an oil capital as well). Both facts are confirmed on the modern emblem of the city, where sturgeons and an oil derrick are depicted. It is Atyrau where numerous photos of expats (working in local offices of Chevron, Agip, BP, etc.) with caviar were often taken about ten years ago. The majority of those photos had the same plot: a table with a big jar of black caviar on it and a happy smiling man, holding a huge tablespoon full of caviar. Times are changing though, and now caviar, even in Atyrau, is not so easy to obtain. They say that nowadays the average price of 1 kg of black caviar in Atyrau is a little bit more than 1000 US dollars, while in Almaty it is already 2000 US dollars. You should also know that commercial fishing for sturgeon is prohibited in the Caspian Sea as of 5 years ago. So, if you think of buying black caviar, be warned it is not a legal product. Poaching is a big industry in the Caspian region, do not support it, even if you want to make one of those notorious photos. There are plenty of other fish roe products that almost replace caviar, so you can still enjoy the tradition!

KAZY

For many people eating horse, a Kazakh nomad's best friend, may sound a bit too cannibalistic. But it is common for people in Kazakhstan, and is surprisingly tasty and very healthy. Kazy, a horse sausage, is mainly a festive meal, so you will definitely see its dark slices at weddings, birthdays and other celebrations. How to cook it? Simply take washed horse intestine and fill it with horse flesh and fat, together with spices (salt, pepper, cumin, and sometimes garlic). The meat is inserted into the intestine together with the rib, so the sausage always has a half-round form. This is then left in a cold place for 2 days or so. Finally kazy is usually boiled (for about 2 hours on a slow fire). It can also be smoked (12-18 hours) or jerked (about a week). In places like the Green Bazaar in Almaty, kazy can be prepared for cooking right in front of you.

TEA PARTY

Tea is undoubtedly one of the main and most universal expressions of Kazakh hospitality. A small bowl with tea is the first thing that is offered to the weary wanderer by every household. Kazakhs generally prefer black tea with, although in the south, closer to Uzbekistan, it is replaced by a green tea. Keep in mind that if someone offers you a cup of tea, you should not take the phrase too literally. Be prepared for the fact that one is not limited to serving just tea, with many visitors anticipating a warm brew being served vodka or koumiss instead. Tea is often supplied at the beginning of the meal. The traveller will be offered a wide choice of dishes to go with their tea such as candy, cookies, halvah, nuts, pastries, dried fruits, baursaks and oil, as well as a bunch of other dishes to keep the guest busy while the host prepares the main meal.

History.

ABAI PLACES

Many believe eastern Kazakhstan to be the spiritual centre of the country. This opinion has arisen because it was here that the most famous Kazakh poet and philosopher, Abai Kunanbayev, lived. As the author of poems and philosophical works, a talented translator, composer, educator and social activist, Abai was the founder of modern Kazakh written literature.

There is also the Zhidebay tract at the spurs of the Shyngystau Ridge in the Abai district of East Kazakhstan. This is where the family residence of Kunanbayev is located, which was bequeathed to Abai in 1884. It is in Zhidebai that he wrote most of his poems and translations. The same house is now a museum dedicated to Abai with interesting historical expositions. In the last century, the Zhidebai memorial complex, "Abai-Shakarim," was built, underneath which lay the remains of Abai and his relatives, some of whom, in particular, the poet and philosopher Shakarim Kudaiberdiev, also contributed to the Kazakh culture.

GREAT GAME OF SHOKAN VALIKHANOV

Shokan Valikhanov went down in history as a great explorer of Central Asia, discovering a virtually unknown world surrounding the city of Kashgar. He carried out many expeditions to the region, studying data on the history, geography, and ethnography of the many peoples who inhabited this land in the middle of the 19th century. Valikhanov became one of the first Kazakhs to receive a European education and took the opportunity to combine modern knowledge with ancient traditions. During his short life (he died before he reached 30), Valikhanov managed to master many professions: traveller, writer, ethnographer, historian, geographer, military servant, artist, cartographer, and even intelligence officer – becoming a key participant of the famous Great Game rivalry between the British and Russian empires for dominance in Central Asia. In Kazakhstan, many places are associated with the name of Valikhanov. These are Semey, Almaty, the foothills of the Altyn-Emel and the mountain passes of the Tien Shan.

215

93

100 EXPERIENCES OF MODERN KAZAKHSTAN

AISHA-BIBI MAUSOLEUM

Written sources do not contain any information about the history of the mausoleum of Aisha-Bibi, situated not far from Taraz. Only a legend exists about the romantic love of a brave soldier, Karakhan, and the beauty of Aisha and her nurse called Babaji Khatun. The most popular version of the legend ends with Aisha's death from a snake's bite, leading to Karakhan, in his grief, erecting a mausoleum in memory of his beloved and the dedication of her nurse, who promised to take care of the grave until her death.

The fame of the Aisha-Bibi mausoleum has brought its decoration: the entire surface of the building is a solid terra-cotta coating depicted with rich and diverse patterns. Babaji Khatun Mausoleum, located next to the first mausoleum, by contrast, is characterized by its simplicity of architectural composition. The local population has special affection for both mausoleums. The romantic aura surrounding them is obvious and the reason that it has become a custom for newly married couples to come here during the wedding ceremony and walk counter-clockwise past the mausoleums. People say that this act, preformed while praying, will save the couple from poverty and other ailments.

GOLDEN MAN OF ISSYK

The Golden Man is one of the most popular symbols of Kazakhstan and one of the starting points for the new identity of Kazakhs. The name of the Issyk burial mound, where it was found, has become known around the world as the site of one of the greatest archaeological finds of the Saka (Scythian) period dating back to the 5th and 6th centuries B.C. Located on the outskirts of the town of Issyk, 50 kilometres east of Almaty, the burial mound was excavated in 1969. Here archaeologists discovered a grave lined with fir logs on the floor on which laid the remains of a Scythian warrior's ceremonial clothing, completely covered with 4,000 gold ornamental components. The headdress is tall and pointed, decorated with images of winged horses, snow leopards, mountain goats and birds. This warrior is likely to have been a prince, although his identity remains unknown.

Today, the site of discovery houses an open-air museum of "Saki mounds". The excavation of ancient burial grounds is not yet complete, which allows visitors the opportunity to watch them take place or even take part in them. Today the original Golden Man is kept in a state depository and copies are exhibited in virtually all the country's major historical museums.

THE MAUSOLEUM OF KHODJA AKHMED YASSAVI

The land of Southern Kazakhstan is rich in holy places, revered by Muslims and regarded as places of pilgrimage. However, the Mausoleum of Khodja Akhmed Yassavi, a famous poet, philosopher and preacher of Islam who became leader of the Sufi Order "Yassaviya", takes an honourable first place among them. Yassavi was one of those people who brought a "soft" and tolerant version of Islam to the steppe, which still prevails in Central Asia. This form of Islam did not promote or lead to the religious wars and witch-hunting seen in other offshoots.

The Mausoleum of Akhmed Yassavi, built in Turkestan at the turn of 13th-14th centuries, by order of Tamerlane himself, includes a number of areas, the most important of which are the gurkhana (tomb) of Ahmed, the "Jamaatkhana" meeting hall, a mosque, a mixture of large and small "aksaray" meeting areas, a "kitabkhana" (library), and "askhana" (dining room). The Jamaatkhana is considered the central hall and connects to the rest of the premises. At the centre is a huge ceremonial cauldron, a symbol of unity and hospitality. The Jamaatkhana is covered with the largest dome in Central Asia, which is 18.2 metres in diameter and the complex is deservedly a UNESCO World Heritage Site.

96

MANGYSTAU
UNDERGROUND "MOSQUES"

The legendary underground "mosques" in the Caspian region Magystau are the caves of preachers from the Sufi branch of Islam, rooted in these parts during the 14th century. They were cut into the limestone rocks in order to house Sufi teachers, their families, and students. Today, they are places of pilgrimage.

The Shakpak-Ata "Mosque", located on the Tub-Karagan peninsula, northeast of Fort-Shevchenko, is considered the most interesting place in cave architecture in Western Kazakhstan. The cave has been carved into the shape of a Latin cross consisting of four chambers, supported by four columns with capitals. On the portal and the inner walls of the underground mosque there are many inscriptions, images of animals and glyphs. Among the inscriptions a Sufi poem stands out, referring to the impermanence of the world and shortness of human life.

Interesting examples of similar architecture can also be seen at the Shopan-Ata mosque, which is surrounded by the largest ancient necropolis in Kazakhstan and located in the settlement of Seneca, more than 200 kilometres from the city of Aktau. This mosque was built by one of the disciples of St. Khodja Akhmed Yassavi, who also built the Becket Ata mosque and the mosque in the chalk rocks at Oglandy in the Western part of the Ustyurt Plateau.

97

PETROGLYPHS TAMGALY

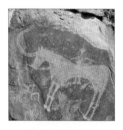

Bronze and Iron age rock carvings and images were found in the Tamgaly ravine, located in the south-eastern part of the Chu-Ili Mountains, in the late 1950s. Despite the fact that many petroglyphs have been found in different parts of Kazakhstan since, these have become the true classics. The name Tamgaly in Kazakh and various other Turkic languages means the "painted or marked place." The most famous images discovered show divine or shamanic figures with circular halos "of sun" around their heads. These images have become popular symbols in modern Kazakhstan.

The Tamgaly area covers approximately 10 kilometres and has nearly 5,000 paintings across the whole site filled with a number of side canyons to explore. Many different eras in the history of the human development are present including the Middle and Late Bronze ages (14th-12th centuries B.C.) and the Saks, Usun, and Turkic periods. Until recently, next to the main canyon, a military training ground was located. Sadly the ignorant manoeuvres of the armed forces over the years have led to significant destruction of many of the stone slabs containing petroglyphs. Today the site is included in the UNESCO list of World Cultural Heritage Sites and is protected, although previous restoration attempts have lost some of the authenticity of this former site of worship.

TEREKTY-AULIYE ROCK CARVINGS

The petroglyphs of Terekty-Auliye relate to the Bronze Age (second millennium B.C.), and are found dotted on flat granite outcrop located 80 kilometres northeast of Zhezkazgan. The most prevalent motifs are associated with animals, mostly horses, camels and oxen. The drawings are a reflection of the nomadic life of ancient people with stories devoted to hunting, wild animals and images that show them worshiping the sun. The technique used in drawing the image is of special interest to scientists studying early man. First the contour of the image was drawn and then the picture around the contour is smoothed with pebbles. There are many legends associated with Terekty Auliye which bring all manner of pilgrims to visit. To the west of the granite paintings there is an open-air museum for those interested in Kazakh Mazars, the resting places of noblemen and cultural figures from the 9th century.

227

METEORITE CRATER ZHAMANSHIN

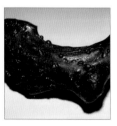

To the north-west of the Small Aral Sea, lies a site that is popular among geologists across the world. Approximately one million years ago, a huge meteorite fell there with such force that the energy released was the equivalent to the explosion of multiple nuclear bombs. Geological deposits, buried deep beneath the earth's surface, were suddenly brought up into the atmosphere in the tumultuous impact. The diameter of the crater, according to recent data, is about 13 miles, and its depth today is approximately 300 metres. Zhamanshin is a unique place where you can discover fossils of molluscs and corals right under your feet, as well as tektites – black or dark green glassy formations whose, origin has been the subject of much dispute among scientists for more than a century. Some believe that tektites are terrestrial rocks that melted again during the explosion; others lean towards an extra-terrestrial origin of these materials, suggesting that these substances are the components of a comet's nucleus. Chemically, tektites do not resemble any well-known terrestrial and extra-terrestrial materials. The debate continues.

SHUNAK METEORITE CRATER

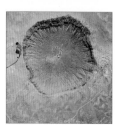

40 kilometres to the west of the Moiynty railway station, in the south-eastern part of Qaraghandy Province, is one of the most interesting natural monuments of extra-terrestrial origin – the Shunak Meteorite Crater. The crater is believed to have formed about 12 million years ago as a result of the impact of a huge meteorite, which is thought to have obliterated all living creatures for several thousand kilometres. Shunak is 3100 metres in diameter (which is two and a half times the diameter of the famous Arizona crater in the U.S.) and 400 metres deep. Many believe that this is a mystical place with unusual powers, which brings all types of curious visitors to see it as well as its cousin, the Zhamanshin crater northeast of the Small Aral Sea.

MAP OF KAZAKHSTAN

CONTENTS

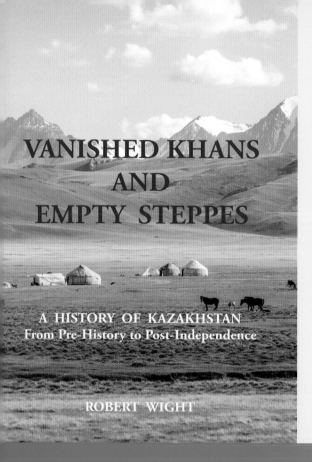

VANISHED KHANS
AND
EMPTY STEPPES

A HISTORY OF KAZAKHSTAN
From Pre-History to Post-Independence

ROBERT WIGHT

The book opens with an outline of the history of Almaty, from its nineteenth-century origins as a remote outpost of the Russian empire, up to its present status as the thriving second city of modern-day Kazakhstan. The story then goes back to the Neolithic and early Bronze Ages, and the sensational discovery of the famous Golden Man of the Scythian empire. The transition has been difficult and tumultuous for millions of people, but Vanished Khans and Empty Steppes illustrates how Kazakhstan has emerged as one of the world's most successful post-communist countries.

VANISHED KHANS AND EMPTY STEPPES by Robert Wight (2014)
Hardback / Paperback
ISBN: 978-0-9930444-0-3
RRP: £9.95

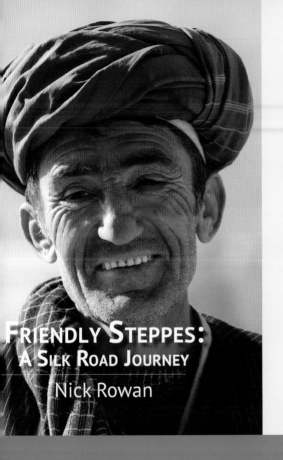

This is the chronicle of an extraordinary adventure that led Nick Rowan to some of the world's most incredible and hidden places. Intertwined with the magic of 2,000 years of Silk Road history, he recounts his experiences coupled with a remarkable realisation of just what an impact this trade route has had on our society as we know it today. Containing colourful stories, beautiful photography and vivid characters, and wrapped in the local myths and legends told by the people Nick met and who live along the route, this is both a travelogue and an education of a part of the world that has remained hidden for hundreds of years.

FRIENDLY STEPPES:
A SILK ROAD JOURNEY

Nick Rowan

FRIENDLY STEPPES: A SILK ROAD JOURNEY by Nick Rowan
Hardback / Paperback
ISBN: 978-0-9927873-4-9
RRP: £17.50

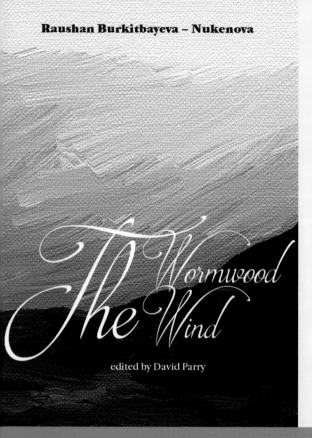

Raushan Burkitbayeva – Nukenova

The Wormwood Wind

edited by David Parry

This candid poetry collection is clearly th[e] literary outpouring of a planetary citize[n.] A woman equally at home on the Stepp[es] of Central Asia as much as the Capit[al] cities of Europe. To my mind, a far fro[m] trivial verity once we recognise the inna[te] femininity of her versification. Similar[ly] to Sappho (5th Century BC), Nuken[o]va allows everyone access into a woma[n'] world, wherein seductive complexities [of] thought becomes manifest through w[it] and rhetoric. Admittedly, her images a[re] often sharp-carefully elaborated for the[ir] own jovial sake.

THE WORMWOOD WIND by Raushan Burkitbaeva-Nukenova
Hardback
ISBN: 978-1-910886-12-0
RRP: £14.95

Available on www.amazon.com / www.amazon.co.uk

THE PLIGHT
OF A POSTMODERN HUNTER
EDITED BY DAVID PARRY

CHINGIZ AITMATOV
MUKHTAR SHAKHANOV

This edition is Mukhtar Shahanov's authorized reprint of Walter May translation of "The Plaint of the Hunter Above the Abyss" book initially published by Atamura in 1998. This is a book-dialogue between two famous pundits, the renowned Kirghizian novelist Chingiz Aitmatov and the legendary Kazakh poet Mukhtar Shakhanov - defending their fundamental faith in the spiritual resources of each and every human being. As such, they explore the moral significance of endlessly recurrent existential dislocations characterising everyone's sense of Personalist encounter with the world around them. A discussion taking them through the riddles posed by ancient philosophies, Turkic histories, African priest-magicians, two-fanged poisonous fish, modern zombism, and Genghis Khan's Golden Hoard: all the way to power politics in the Kremlin, the risks taken by Premier Mikhail Gorbachev as well as the duties, not to mention the obligations, of writers serving in the sphere of international public affairs.

THE PLIGHT OF A POSTMODERN HUNTER by Chingiz Aitmatov
& Mukhtar Shahanov
Hardback
ISBN: 978-1-910886-11-3
RP: £24.95

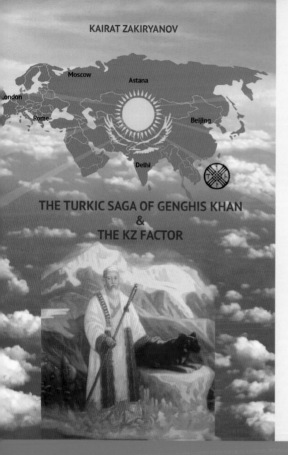

KAIRAT ZAKIRYANOV

THE TURKIC SAGA OF GENGHIS KHAN
&
THE KZ FACTOR

An in-depth study of Genghis Khan from
Kazakh perspective, The Turkic Saga of Geng
his Khan presupposes that the great Mo
gol leader and his tribal setting had more i
common with the ancestors of the Kazakl
than with the people who today identify
Mongols. This idea is growing in currency i
both western and eastern scholarship and
challenging both old Western assumption
and the long-obsolete Soviet perspective. Th
is an academic work that draws on many Cen
tral Asian and Russian sources and often h
a Eurasianist bias - while also paying atten
tion to new accounts by Western authors suc
as Jack Weatherford and John Man. It bea
the mark of an independent, unorthodox an
passionate scholar.

THE TURKIC SAGA OF GENGHIS KHAN AND THE KZ FACTOR
Hardback   by Dr.Kairat Zakiryanov
ISBN: 978-0-9927873-7-0
RRP: £9.95

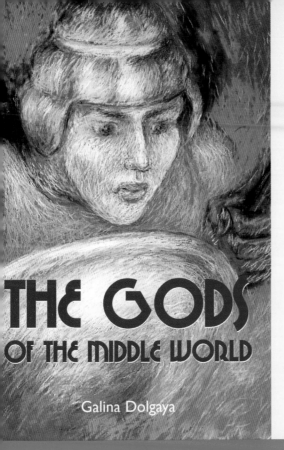

THE GODS
OF THE MIDDLE WORLD

Galina Dolgaya

The Gods of the Middle World tells the story of Sima, a student of archaeology for whom the old lore and ways of the Central Asian steppe peoples are as vivid as the present. When she joints a group of archaeologists in southern Kazakhstan, asking all the time whether it is really possible to 'commune with the spirits', she soon discovers the answer first hand, setting in motion events in the spirit world that have been frozen for centuries. Meanwhile three millennia earlier, on the same spot, a young woman and her companion struggle to survive and amend wrongs that have caused the neighbouring tribe to take revenge. The two narratives mirror one another, and Sima's destiny is to resolve the ancient wrongs in her own lifetime and so restore the proper balance of the forces of good and evil.

ODS OF THE MIDDLE WORLD by G. Dolgaya
ıperback
BN: 978-0-9574807-9-7
RP: £9.95

HERTFORDSHIRE PRESS

Available on www.amazon.com / www.amazon.co.uk

Hotel "Kazakhstan" is a unique historic monument of Almaty and a sample
monumental, solid and reliable Soviet architecture . Hotel "Kazakhstan" is
of the few hotels in the world which has become an integral part of the cit

Dostyk Avenue 52\2, Kazakhstan Hotel, Telephone +7 727 291 91 01

Traditions of hospitality and modern comfort!

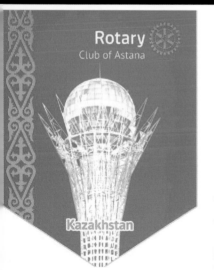

Uzbekistan -
Wows you!

We offer following services:
✓ Hotel accommodation,
✓ Transport services,
✓ Visa support,
✓ Guide and translator services

HAVAS TOUR SERVICE

Contact us:
150, M. Ulugbek street 140107
Samarkand, Republic of Uzbekistan
Tel: +998 90 6558088; +998 90 6550500
Fax: +998 66 2340089
www.samarkand-tours.com
info@samarkand-tours.com

Havas
Tour Service